weelicious

weelicious

140 FAST, FRESH, AND EASY RECIPES

Catherine McCord

WM
WILLIAM MORROW
An Imprint of HarperCollinsPublishers

**When you see this icon next to a recipe,
check out weeliciousbook.com/extras for
step-by-step cooking videos with Catherine!**

The photographs on pages 72, 81, 106, 111, and 116 were taken by Jonathan Gordon.

HarperCollins books may be purchased for educational, business, or sales promotional use. For information please write: Special Markets Department, HarperCollins Publishers, 10 East 53rd Street, New York, NY 10022.

FIRST EDITION

Designed by Kris Tobiassen

Library of Congress Cataloging-in-Publication Data

McCord, Catherine.
    Weelicious : 150 fast, fresh, and easy recipes / Catherine McCord. — 1st ed.
        p. cm.
    Includes index.
    ISBN 978-0-06-207844-5 (hardback)
 1. Quick and easy cooking. I. Title.
    TX833.5.M427 2012
    641.5'55—dc23
                                                    2012018048

12 13 14 15 16 ID/RRD 10 9 8 7 6 5 4 3 2 1

For Kenya and Chloe, without whom
there would be no weelicious.

And for JG, without whom
there would be no Kenya and Chloe.

contents

Preface: Why No Parent Should Fear the Kitchen ix

Introduction: Our Kids Can Be Great Eaters! xi

PART 1: GETTING STARTED 1

from the first bite: there's an easier way 3

Good Habits Start from the First Few Bites 3

The Science of Your Child's Taste Buds 4

No More Food Fights 6

Stop Sneaking! Let Kids Know What They're Eating 8

"My Kid Will Only Eat Chicken Nuggets!" 10

"This Doesn't Taste Healthy . . ." 12

Just Because You Don't Like Spinach Doesn't Mean Your Kids Won't 14

shopping: setting yourself up for success 17

Food Shopping with the Kids 17

Moms and Dads Beware! 18

Shopping for High-Quality Food at the Lowest Prices Possible 19

Cooking Healthy Doesn't Have to
Break the Bank (or Even Come Close!) 20

Organic vs. Non-Organic and the "Dirty Dozen" 21

cooking: turning passive eaters into active ones...........25

Getting Your Kids Involved in Cooking..............................25

The Work Pays Off!...31

You're Not a Short-Order Cook: How Not to
Be a Slave to Your Kids in the Kitchen.............................33

Your Basic Kitchen Gear...33

Weelicious Cooking Staples...36

eating: secrets revealed!...........39

Giving Kids Some Choice...39

Making Food Fun...40

The Family That Eats Together 41

PART 2: RECIPES...........43

baby purees...........44

breakfast...........58

soup...........89

dips, sauces, and salsas...........102

snacks...........120

dinner...........154

sides...........209

desserts...........230

drinks...........256

Acknowledgments...267

Index..270

why no parent
should fear the kitchen

If you bought this book or are flipping through it in the bookstore, chances are you're in need of help.

For countless moms like us, the task of cooking for our families can feel like a hopeless exercise—an incredibly frustrating experience that creates all sorts of anxiety and conflict. I'm very familiar with the inner mom-ologues: "Why can't I make just one meal that satisfies *everyone* in our family?" "Why won't my kids eat *anything* I make them?" "If only I could inspire my little ones to eat healthy (let alone eat *something*)." Similarly, if you're anything like the readers of my website, weelicious, the kitchen is not a place where you always exude confidence, and if one word on the cover of this book persuaded you to pick it up, I'd wager it's "easy." Well, you'll be happy to know that *you* are the reason I wrote this book.

I consider myself to be a pretty good cook. I spent my formative years in the South—where cooking is serious business—in a family full of food lovers who were always in the kitchen either cooking, eating, or gathering, and for whom our weekly Sunday night family dinner was a sacred event not to be missed. From a very early age my mom and grandparents exposed me to food and its relationship to the world around me, taking me to U-Pick farms and exposing me to their love of gardening. That doesn't mean I always ate healthy. My grandmother's most cherished cooking staple was not a bottle of olive oil or a pepper mill but a mason jar full of bacon grease that sat in a place of honor next to the stovetop and was the fundamental ingredient in everything she cooked.

In my teens and early twenties I traveled the world modeling and fell even more deeply in love with food, getting to experience the different flavors and cuisines of exotic and far-flung locales. Modeling was a privilege and it had its obvious benefits, but it hardly fulfilled my lifelong aspirations. However, it allowed me to save enough to put myself through culinary school, where I learned a lot and had the opportunity to work in some of the great kitchens of New York and Los Angeles. After cultivating an intimate knowledge of food over three decades, you probably couldn't find a person better prepared to cook for her new baby boy. Right?

Wrong.

It quickly became apparent that the one thing I *didn't* learn after all those years was that cooking for babies (and kids) is a different ball of wax *entirely*. Here I was, an experienced cook who knew my way around every corner of the kitchen and believed I could cook for any occasion, yet when I had my first child, I did not have *a clue* how to feed him. I'm not kidding. I was completely paralyzed. So, if that was my experience, how is the person with *no* cooking background supposed to feed their kids?

The truth is, *none of us* is prepared for what we should be feeding these little creatures when they enter our lives, let alone how to go about doing it. It's a scary predicament for any mom to find herself in. Our first instinct as parents is to provide for our children in every way imaginable, and few needs are more important to meet than nourishment. When I had my son, most of the new moms I knew had never stepped foot into a kitchen before, and they all were experiencing the same anxiety as me. So my goal when I started weelicious became "How can I make cooking as easy as possible for my friends?"

Because if my recipes will work for them, they should work for everyone.

Not convinced? Maybe you're thinking, *This book isn't for me. I've barely logged a total of two hours in a kitchen before having kids, and Catherine has had years of experience. She must have known what she was doing.* I really didn't. What I quickly discovered when I started weelicious was that everything I needed to learn about cooking for babies and kids was just starting. I literally had to go back to the basics for everything I would make, but it had to be *easy*.

At the end of the day, I have always considered myself a lazy cook. No matter who it is I'm feeding—my kids, family, or friends—if what I'm making is not simple to prepare, I'm not making it. And why should I? Why should you? Why should any of us spend more time in the kitchen than we need to—especially if we're not having fun doing it? As important as food is, between trying to raise kids, work, pay bills, and run a household, none of us has the luxury of time we had before bringing these little wonders into the world. So for every recipe I create, I focus on convenience and using the minimum amount of ingredients to create the maximum amount of flavor.

If I haven't scared you off yet, I promise that your life can change for the better if you buy into my philosophy. Spend just a little bit of time with this cookbook and you'll discover that cooking for your family is not only easy but something you'll look forward to. Really.

our kids can be great eaters!

When I had my son, Kenya, I didn't know how to start educating myself about how and what to feed him. So I took my past knowledge, did extensive research, and started blogging every day about my experiences making homemade baby food. I had a blast, and in the beginning, my intention was to focus solely on babies, but as my son got older, so did the children of weelicious readers. The number of e-mails and comments I received grew daily, and the common refrain I kept hearing was, "My kids won't eat anything I make them!"

Adapting to the needs of my readers and living the challenges presented by my own son, I quickly discovered that the methods required to feed babies, toddlers, and kids were very different from the ones we employ to feed adults. Delicious food alone doesn't cut it. Kids experience the world of food quite unlike we grown-ups do, and so one must be sensitive to everything from shape, to color, to texture, to taste when cooking for them. I not only had to develop recipes but *strategies* for how to present food to kids.

And while most moms approach feeding their families with the best of intentions, the pitfall most of us fall into is trying to please everyone in our families—or what I call "short-order cook syndrome." This condition occurs when moms, in an effort to get everyone to eat at mealtime, get stuck making something different for each member of the family—one thing for their baby, another dish for their "demanding" toddler, and yet something else for themselves and their spouse. It takes all the joy out of food, and that makes me sad.

Once you become a parent, the subject of food never goes away. Having to provide three meals and one to two snacks a day, *what to eat* is constantly on a mother's mind. Just figuring out what to make your kids is hard enough. Factor in trying to navigate each child's unique and ever-changing relationship with food and it can drive even the most level-headed mom or dad crazy. After years of experience with my own little ones and talking with thousands of parents and their own children, I have developed tips,

strategies, and ideas that make moms look forward to preparing their child's food and inspire the pickiest little eaters to get excited about the next meal to come.

When they first approach me, many mothers begin by confiding, "I'm a terrible mother. How is it that I don't know how to cook for my child?" First, we moms have to stop blaming ourselves and realize that this disconnect many of us have with cooking is not our fault. We are of a generation that grew up consuming a considerable amount of drive-thru, processed, and prepackaged food. Unlike our grandmothers' generation (and the generations before theirs), whose relationship to food was cultivated almost entirely at the elbow of their mothers,

aunts, and grandmothers, many of us grew up more familiar with mass-produced food and therefore had little exposure to the inner workings of our own kitchens. The use of artificial preservatives and stabilizers coupled with more women entering the workforce meant that our generation spent disproportionately less time than our grandmothers did in the kitchen. Most moms today never really learned how to cook, but that doesn't mean you can't start now. We need to reconnect with our inner mom—and with just a few simple cooking techniques, we can.

When you make something for your family and they like it, that's a *huge* accomplishment. You *will* be able to make these meals and have the satisfaction of hearing, "That's *awesome*, Mom."

PART I
GETTING STARTED

from the first bite: there's an easier way

good habits start from the first few bites

One of the greatest gifts you can give your baby from their very first bite of food is an introduction to a wide variety of fresh fruits and vegetables. Exposing children to a diverse spectrum of tastes, flavors, and textures allows them to fully experience the world of food and get used to being open to new things. In the words of a friend of mine, "You want to mold the clay when it's fresh and pliable." The more diversity you offer your baby early on, the more he knows and is comfortable with, and that will pay off down the line.

I vividly remember the looks on each of my kids' faces when they experienced their first tastes of the homemade baby food I prepared for them. It was amazing: me putting the spoons to their mouths for the first time, them looking intensely at the food and trying to figure out what it was, each of them taking their first tastes and encountering a flavor and texture beyond the milk they had been consuming out of a boob or bottle for the previous six months. They'd been shown a part of the world that, until that moment, they'd only passively watched others experience. How incredible those moments must be for them! And how magical for my husband and me to experience it all with our children. This should be one of the highlights of parenthood, because you're offering your children knowledge of the foods that will nurture them and help them to grow.

There are no two ways about it: When prepared properly, homemade baby food tastes better and is arguably more nutritious for your baby than anything you can buy in a grocery store, which is designed to sit on a shelf for a year or more. When you also factor in the benefits of knowing exactly what goes into your baby's food and not having to pay a premium for the better brands who use the same high-quality, organic produce you can likely find for less, it's hard to deny the benefits of homemade.

Also, as kids get older, they can become increasingly resistant to changes in their diets (just as they can to changes in their routines, and so on). Children understandably become comfortable with the foods they were offered most often in their first few years. If you've exposed them to a lot of processed foods, it stands to reason that they'll become attached to that manner of eating. Coupled with their ever-burgeoning desire for more independence and control as they get older, children become progressively more hesitant to try new things—even resistant to your efforts. So start molding your clay when it's young and malleable—it will lead to better habits down the road!

Remember these tips as you begin your journey:

- Start with fruits or vegetables? There's no perfect first food to start feeding your baby. I've heard many people say that if you start your baby on fruit, she'll always have a sweet tooth or crave sweets. I've never subscribed to that theory, and there's no scientific proof to support it. The bottom line is that you can't go wrong when you choose fresh, flavorful, real (and in most cases, organic) food.

- Choose what's in season. You can be assured that your homemade baby food will be at its height of nutritional power and freshness when what you use to make it hasn't traveled thousands of miles by ship, truck, or airplane to get to you.

- Every baby is different when it comes to starting solids. It's important to follow your baby's cues as to when he is ready for solids. For most babies, when they start reaching, fussing about, or looking longingly at the food on your plate, it's a good sign that they're ready to take the plunge.

the science of your child's taste buds

I've lost count of the number of times a mom has complained to me, "My son hates [*insert name of food your child despises most*]." Undoubtedly, though, as soon as I ask a mom how many times their little one has tried the dreaded food in question, the answer is once—maybe twice. A seemingly strong aversion to any particular food is enough to make most parents believe they have a picky eater. However, research says that we need to be patient with our children when introducing them to new foods. Getting kids to be great eaters doesn't *literally* start at the first bite. Studies have shown that it can take up to *fifteen times* before a child will start to enjoy a certain food. While that may strike you as a long time, it's a lot shorter than the amount of time (possibly *years*) a kid will spend avoiding a food that he didn't learn to like as a small child.

Understand a bit of the science behind why and how we as humans learn to enjoy certain foods and it all starts to make sense. When a baby is born, he has over *ten thousand* taste buds, significantly more than adults do. Taste buds deteriorate with age, and the ones that remain become less sensitive, but what's key here is that the taste and flavor of what your baby is eating is notably more intense than how that same food tastes to you. When you see your baby try a food for the first time, the expression on his little face in reaction to the explosion of flavor he's tasting says it all: He may find it electrifying, fascinating, and sometimes just plain overwhelming. Your child's first encounters with any food can have a profound effect—both positive and negative—on his current and future enjoyment of it depending on how *you* react, so it's crucial that you're patient and don't leap to conclusions about what your baby likes or doesn't like. And since your baby is completely dependent on you for his exposure to different kinds of food and opportunities to develop a taste for them, if he rejects a certain food today, put it aside and try again tomorrow. And the day after that. And the day after that. I guarantee that one day very soon, you'll be shocked when you see your baby reaching for that very same food you thought he had rejected permanently.

When it comes to the five core tastes—sweet, sour, salty, bitter, and umami (which is difficult to describe but translated roughly as rich savoriness)—no two people are the same in their preferences, and this applies to babies and adults alike. So the more variety you offer your little one, the more chances you're giving them to get excited about food in all its diversity. These preferences will carry through with them for life.

Thinking globally helps keep things in perspective as well. In India kids eat curry and other intense spices; in Mexico most children have a

diet that includes chiles, moles, and other vibrant flavors. Babies and children adapt to whatever culinary environment they're in.

My mother says it took me way more than ten tries before I started enjoying mushrooms as a kid, but before long I was requesting them at dinnertime. I've seen the same thing happen with my own kids. I attribute it to my family's attitude about food. No one ever said to me, "You won't like it" or "You're too young to enjoy this." Similarly, I never would have thought that babies would enjoy something like olives—in fact, I consciously avoided using them in weelicious recipes. But given the chance, my daughter will down a jar of bitter black Kalamatas in minutes, so time and again, I've learned the value of patience, exposure, and checking my preconceived notions at the door.

No matter how patient and diligent you are, you may not have luck getting your child to like everything you expose her to. No one loves every food they've ever tried, so don't be hard on yourself if your best efforts still meet with occasional resistance. Ultimately, your kids are learning that it's good to try new things, and that's an important lesson in life, period.

no more food fights

The first rule of feeding is patience. One thing I've learned preparing twenty-one-plus meals a week, fifty-two weeks a year, is that if you get into a food fight with your kids, no one's going to win, especially you. A lovely day can quickly turn disastrous when a child decides it's time to

exercise her willpower. I know moms who would rather take a punch in the ring from Mike Tyson in his prime than do battle with their little one over eating their dinner. Worse, engaging in battles may help to turn your child away from a food he may learn to love if only given the space and time to do so on his own. It will help you if you're prepared for disappointment (your kid *will* reject things you put lots of love and care into making) and practice your own ability to relinquish control (sometimes you'll just *have* to accept that your kid is not going to eat on your clock).

I've heard from loads of parents who disagree with me and believe that their kids will not eat well without their constant pushing. My fear is that pushing will have far worse consequences. A recent NPR article entitled "To Win Toddler Food Battles, Take a Softer Approach" quoted an interesting study: "Kids who were offered a high-calorie first course chose—on their own—a lower-calorie second course. And those offered a low-calorie first course? They opted for a second course with higher calories. In other words, they self-regulated."

In that same article, Andrea Garber, chief nutritionist for the child obesity program at the University of California, San Francisco, says, "Young children are very, very good at regulating their intake so they are getting the proper amount of calories and fat and carbohydrates and protein for growth—as long as they're offered a healthy range of items." Garber goes on to caution that kids' innate ability to self-regulate their diets can become seriously damaged when parents interfere and try to force them to eat.

Garber discusses another experiment, in which kids were given a meal, followed by the ability to have whatever snacks they desired: The study found that the children with more restrictive mothers ate significantly more cookies and snack food when their mothers weren't present.

It's important to underscore here that if the options you offer your children are healthy ones, kids will naturally get enough nutrition—even if they exercise little control over what they eat. But, as I said earlier, if kids are accustomed to expecting food of little to no nutritional value (or what's more commonly referred to as *junk*), it's a different story. The foods children self-regulate with are only as good as the choices their parents make available to them.

That's not to say any of this is easy. On the whole, my kids are great eaters, but they both also have very strong-willed personalities. Once, when Kenya was around three, I made him one of the more labor-intensive things I've ever prepared for him: one of my childhood favorites, individual chicken pot pies. As I proudly removed the ramekins from the oven, he took one look at them, said, "I don't want that," and walked away. I've worked for some tough chefs and consider myself to have a thick skin in the kitchen, but my feelings were totally hurt by an innocent little kid. Here I was, sharing a piece of my childhood with my son, and he completely snubbed me.

However, knowing how finicky and temperamental kids can be, I decided not to push Kenya and waited to see what happened if I didn't engage. I let him continue to play in the kitchen, and about fifteen minutes later I saw him wander over to where the pies were cooling, take a fork, and investigate his little pot pie. He took one bite, turned to me, and said, "I love it!" No joke. He went from unwilling to try it to loving it in a matter of minutes, and I didn't have to do anything but be patient. When it comes to kids and eating, if there's one thing I've learned time and again, it's that pushing new foods on them almost always makes them more resistant to trying them. When you allow kids to discover things for themselves, it affords them ownership over what they eat and a sense of revelation with food that just can't be achieved by cajoling, sneaking, persuading, or begging.

Now, I was lucky that time. Fifteen minutes is not long to wait. Often it will take you more than several attempts before your little one will come around, but whatever you do, *don't push and get into a food fight.* I guarantee that you won't win. The fight isn't worth it, and besides you never know when that breakthrough moment is going to come.

Important to keep in mind: *If your child is reluctant to eat or try a new food, consider the context of the situation. Sometimes the defiant "no" you're hearing at mealtime has nothing to do with what you're serving and everything to do with how your child may be feeling: constipated, sick, tired, teething, cranky from school, or simply* not *hungry at the time you put dinner on the table (which in many cases can be because they're filled up on often unhealthy snacks too close to mealtime). While it can be unbelievably stressful for parents to be confronted with what they perceive as rejec-*tion, in these moments, empathy tends to work better than even the most delicious meal.*

stop sneaking! let kids know what they're eating

As a parent I always try to be straightforward with my kids. That's especially true when it comes to feeding them. I believe most parents aim to do the same with their own children, so it concerns me that the current trend of tricking kids into eating their vegetables by sneaking them into the foods they will eat (like recipes that call for adding pureed spinach and carrots to brownies) has become so popular.

Forget that it's so time-consuming to cook deceptively—why is deception a good thing to practice on our children in any form? What kind of message does that send them? I fully understand that little ones can be fussy and particular about what they eat—trust me, I know firsthand how challenging kids can be. But do we really want a country full of eighteen-year-olds who have no idea they *had* eaten cauliflower for years because it was hidden in their banana bread? We should want children to learn from the first bite they put in their little mouths that fruits and vegetables bring pleasure and will make them strong, healthy, and happy.

Is getting kids to eat their vegetables always easy? No. Can it be a struggle with some kids who are simply predisposed to not liking green food? Yes. But as you'll see in later chapters, the more inclusive you are with your kids, the better your results will be.

Take my friend's son Aidan, for example. Until he was five years old, he refused green vegetables. My friend tried any number of ways to encourage him to try them, but for *years* he would just flat-out say no. As you might expect, my friend was at her wits' end. So, one afternoon, my son and I went over to her house armed with my blender, a bunch of collard greens, a lemon, and some honey and we set up shop in her kitchen. After a few minutes, my friend's son came over to me to ask what I was doing. I replied that I was making something called Super Juice. "Super Juice?" he said. I had his attention. I told him that I needed his help. I took out the collard green leaves and showed him how they were like big green fans he could fan the air with, making the food fun and relatable for him rather than something that was going to be imposed upon him to eat or drink. He got a kick out of fanning my son and his mom. I chopped up all the ingredients and asked the boys to stuff and squeeze everything into the blender—again, this was a fun activity for them. Next, I let Aidan press the power button on the blender so he could excitely whip up everything into a frenzy. There was no "sale" needed after that. For the next thirty minutes Kenya and Aidan ran around the house gulping Super Juice and saying to each other, "Look at my muscles, I'm a superhero!" Now, I'm not suggesting that this technique will work on every child, but I find that when you empower your kids to be a part of the process and get them excited about food, the need to sneak simply melts away.

We parents just want to give our kids the tools to fulfill their potential. When they're not eating the foods we know are so important to their physical and mental development, we get more than a little concerned. Understandably, we may feel the need to resort to sneaking fruits and veggies in order to assure ourselves that they're at least getting what they need. When we do this, though, we're setting up our children for poor eating habits down the road and teaching them that deception is acceptable if it's in service of something we feel is important. If we change our attitudes and try to normalize food by making it fun and more approachable, you'd be amazed at how incredibly kids will relish the opportunity to be included. And in becoming empowered, kids become active in shaping their own futures.

Trust me, the amount of effort you'll put into inspiring your kids to eat certain foods takes a heck of a lot less effort than cooking, pureeing, and stuffing broccoli into a banana bread that will take you two hours to make!

"my kid will only eat chicken nuggets!"

A frequent complaint I hear from moms is that their child will only eat pasta with butter, chicken nuggets, white bread, or Pop-Tarts. Unless your little one has recently gotten his driver's license or figured out how to hot-wire your car and make his way to the store, the foods you have a problem with them eating probably

are things you bought in the first place. I don't want to be the bad guy and tell moms that so many of their mealtime stresses are based on the foods they're buying in the grocery store and at the drive-thru, but the truth is that kids can only eat what we give them. The problem is not that they're aware of these foods but rather that we provide them.

Before you say, "Well, what about the Cheetos he gets at friends' houses," or "My mother-in-law takes her to McDonald's," or "I can't control what they serve at birthday parties"—that's not what I'm talking about, as long as it's in moderation. You can do little to control those things and will only drive yourself crazy (though there's no reason you can't have a gentle conversation with the adult in those situations about offering more nutritious choices, especially in the instances where that person is watching your child on a regular basis and providing her with poor-quality snacks). The main thing to concern yourself with is what goes on under your roof (and car roof). I've yet to hear of a child who stopped eating at home because she was only presented with healthy choices. Kids will eat what you make available to them, so what you serve at home during their formative years will become the norm for them.

By way of illustration, I went to my son's school one day and brought along a bunch of books to read to his class. One of them was a favorite of ours called *Fast Food*, which features photographs of cars, airplanes, trucks, motorcycles, and even submarines made entirely out of fruits and vegetables. It's a really cool book, but it was the kids' reactions that really blew me away. As I read aloud, I asked the kids if they could name the fruits and vegetables used to make each vehicle. I was shocked that *no one* knew what an eggplant or zucchini looked like, and fewer than half of them could identify the other fruits or vegetables in the book, which were as common as mushrooms, cucumbers, cauliflower, and peppers.

But the story doesn't end there. I take great pleasure in packing Kenya's lunch for school (to the extent that I photograph the contents of his lunchbox and post it online daily!). One afternoon, Priya, the mom of Kenya's friend Govind, asked me the name of the purple fruit I had put in Kenya's lunch the previous day. Govind had apparently come home exclaiming, "Kenya had purple fruit in his lunch box! Put some in mine too!" I told Priya the fruit was called dragon fruit and where she could buy it. A week later, I decided to bring some dragon fruit to Kenya's class. I cut it up for them and watched a bunch of kids who had never before seen an eggplant or zucchini devour this odd-looking fruit whose name they had giggled about upon hearing it. Of course some of the kids were dubious at first, but the two simple acts of me offering it without pushing and them seeing their peers enjoy it created a classroom full of four-year-olds happily eating dragon fruit.

Or consider the story of weelicious reader Cindy, whose kids were accustomed to a steady diet of boxed and freezer-section processed foods. She was tired of it. When Cindy switched to buying only whole foods two years ago, her kids were skeptical. But, she said, "I kept at it, including them in the process of picking out veggies at the market, taking them to tour farms, and having them help cook at dinner. I find that when they are involved in the process, they want to at least try the Brussels sprouts they made—even if they eventually decide they don't like them."

I've received a lot of testimonials like Cindy's, and they only reinforce my conviction that there's no eater so picky that he can't make progress and become a good, or even great, eater. I'm not saying that your kid will eat every food in the world after you read this book, but I guarantee that if you cut down on giving her McDonald's, chicken nuggets, and mac and cheese at every meal, and instead help her get excited about a variety of nutritious foods, your supposedly picky eater will suddenly become the kid who says, "more Baked Zucchini Coins (page 229), please" or looks forward to making Red Beet and White Bean Hummus (page 104) together.

We're always looking for magic bullets, and the truth is, there are none. If you want to do well in school, you study; if you want to lose weight, you exercise and eat healthy; if you want to be a good piano player, you practice. So it stands to reason that if you want your kids to eat well, you have to set them up for success. When kids eat poorly, it's because *we* allow them to. I hate to be the bearer of bad news, but I think it's the truth. I'm not trying to lay blame on anyone—except maybe the companies that choose to offer our kids unhealthy choices to make a bigger profit—but if you stop buying the bad stuff (and lead by example by eating well yourself), your kids will eat less of it. Simple.

"this doesn't taste healthy . . ."

The most common misperception I hear about cooking healthy, and why I find so many parents resistant to trying it for their kids, is that healthy food doesn't taste as good as the additive-filled and fat-rich food they're used to eating and grew up on. I would argue the exact opposite. I'm no stranger to the pleasures of a good bacon cheeseburger, but fresh, healthy food simply tastes better. It's just that many of us aren't used to tasting the delicious flavors of food as nature intended them. Our palates have become conditioned to the amount of salt, sugar, and additives in the foods we've been eating all our lives. Time and again I hear from parents who don't believe they'll ever be capable of eating well because the taste of a plain vegetable or a slice of whole grain bread is so unappealing to them. We need time for our palates to acclimate to a pure, wholesome, and unprocessed place.

When I was growing up in Kentucky, we ate dinner as a family every night. My mother always put a fruit, vegetable, carbohydrate, and protein on our plates to offer us a balanced meal. I found nothing unusual about eating salad, vegetables, or other unprocessed foods, because it was all I knew.

Now, contrast that with one of my closest girlfriends, who believed until her late teens that peas came from a can (she thought the same about salmon!). A diet consisting of little more than processed and prepackaged foods was all she knew, and she perceived it as not only normal but healthy. My friend admits that it took

the thrill of victory

One of the greatest joys about the weelicious website is the dialogue I'm able to have with my readers. Whether they're new moms, veteran moms, or moms-to-be, I cherish and am always inspired by these amazing women's stories, questions, and above all, feedback. I've included some of their comments below and alongside many of the recipes throughout the book. To me, their stories reflect what kindred spirits we moms are and read like words of encouragement, something we can always use in the kitchen!

PAMELA: I'm a stay-at-home mom of a sixteen-month-old and a nine-year-old. I can honestly say my nine-year-old has tried more new things in this last year than probably her whole life. I also *love* seeing the kids I babysit for light up at things they never thought they would like, with the help of your recipes! We've weaned our house off of all processed/boxed foods. My #1 rule for shopping is, "If I can make it, I can't buy it."

SABRINA: I found your site when I got pregnant with my daughter and my husband and I were talking about making baby food when the time comes. I ended up using some of your recipes with my Brownie unit (seven- and eight-year-olds), and they *love* them. We have some really picky girls, and the parents are shocked (and very happy!) when the girls come home asking for foods they never would have eaten before!

MARY: After my second child started eating solid foods, I wanted to find a variety of healthy recipes for her because my son (who's five) was so picky right from the beginning! I think it was partly my fault because I didn't offer that much variety, so he ate the beige toddler diet. After trying some of your recipes, I can say that though he's still my picky one, they both eat a much better variety of foods. His favorite lately is the spinach muffins! I could've never dreamed of him eating anything with spinach!

ERICA: I found your site when I started staying home and decided to start really cooking, and I love the fact that you can turn anything into something healthy and better for you, and it will taste better than the bad version, too! My kids are amazing eaters and have loved everything I've made off your site, but I was shocked that my husband actually enjoys most of the recipes, too! He's the picky eater, but he and the kids can go through a double batch of your zucchini muffins in two days, and I was really surprised by how much they love the Green Smoothie. You've really opened my eyes to all the nasty chemicals and overprocessed foods!

her until her early thirties, encouraged by lots of prodding by many of our friends, to start eating healthier whole foods, such as fish and fresh vegetables. She's one of the smartest people I know, but it still took her a long time to realize the toll the awful food patterns of her childhood had taken on her body (she was overweight and had low energy and high cholesterol) and the need to reprogram her thinking.

To me, these two stories demonstrate that if you offer your family healthy food, that's what they'll develop a taste for and accept as normal. Conversely, if you offer them canned, boxed, and jarred foods packed with tons of preservatives and additives, then that's what they'll develop a taste for. It all comes down to providing your kids with choice and knowledge.

Helping our children develop that palate at a young age is truly our gift to them. That's part of the reason I urge parents to start making homemade baby food from day one, so that kids can get used to the natural flavors of fresh foods instead of the additive-filled alternatives.

My daughter and I went to a birthday party one time, and when the birthday cake came out, all the other kids clustered around to get their pieces while my daughter was perched by the crudité plate, chowing down on cherry tomatoes, cucumber slices, and sugar snap peas. That's not meant to be boastful—I offer sweets to my kids, and many are the times when both my kids go nuts for cake and cookies. The point is, more times than not, my son and daughter gravitate to the healthy stuff, not because it's healthy or I'm prodding them to, but simply because it's what they've developed a taste for over time.

If you can make the leap of faith and commit that you're going to offer everyone in your house a variety of nutritious foods to eat (yes, that means you too, Mom and Dad), you'll be surprised that those kids you once labeled picky eaters aren't so picky after all.

just because you don't like spinach doesn't mean your kids won't

Okay, I admit it. There are a few foods that I don't like. I don't know many people—even famous chefs—who like to eat *everything*. Raw onions are one of my aversions. But take my son, Kenya. The child could live on raw onions, white and red, if I allowed him to. When he was just two-and-a-half years old, we went to a birthday party with a buffet table. On one end was a platter stacked with kid-friendly buttermilk pancakes. On the platter next to it were parent-friendly bagels, smoked salmon, and piles of sliced raw onions that made me want to cry just looking at them. I got caught up talking to someone, and when I turned around, there was my son, eating fistful after fistful of raw onions.

Then there's Chloe and olives. Whenever my in-laws come to town, I always buy olives in lots of colors, flavors, and sizes for my father-in-law, Sonny, who can't get enough of them. When Chloe was eighteen months old, I walked into the den to find her propping herself up at the coffee table and stuffing olives into her mouth (yes, she should have been better supervised!). My first thought was, *Oh no, she's going to choke!*, followed almost immediately by, *She's eating olives??* To this day Chloe would be happy to eat an entire jar of olives in one sitting and then chase them down by drinking every drop of the bitter, briny liquid they came in. A common refrain from her at our dinner table is "more olive." It would never have occurred to me that she'd like something as strong-tasting as olives, but it was a lesson in the power of preconceived notions. I'm so glad to have learned this lesson early on—and not deprived her of years of the sheer pleasure of eating olives.

Understandably, parents have a habit of making food and culinary decisions for their kids based on their own likes and dislikes. I'm no different. When cooking for our family, of course I want to make things that I think everyone will enjoy, but to be fair, they're usually things that *I* like. It's important when you're making foods at home, or even when you're ordering out, to keep an open mind and allow your kids to try a variety of foods, even the things you may turn your nose up at. For example, I never make lamb. In fact, I cringe when I even hear the word "lamb." But one night I decided to check my aversion at the door and buy some baby lamb chops for the kids to try. I was convinced that one of my kids, if not both of them, had inherited my intense distaste for it, but I refrained from comment, held my breath, seared a couple, and put them out. You can imagine my surprise when I saw both kids *devouring* them, cleaning the meat right off of the bone!

One summer when Kenya was around two, I had a picnic dinner with him at the park. A bunch of neighborhood dads and their kids were also there, and one of the things I was feeding Kenya—some steamed okra—caught the attention of one of the dads. Here's how the conversation went:

Dad A: What's that green stuff?
Me: It's okra.
Dad A: What's okra?
Dad B: It's a vegetable that people eat in the South. It's really slimy.

At this point, Dad A's gorgeous little girl with big blue eyes walked up, staring at Kenya and me as if to say, "Can I try some?"

Me (to the little girl): Would you like some?
Dad A: She won't like it.
Me: Do you mind it if I offer her some?
Dad A: I'm telling you she won't like it, but okay.

The girl's dad was right. She didn't like it . . . she *loved* it! His little girl ate not one, not two, but six pieces of okra. I've given okra to several other kids with great success, and Kenya, well, he could eat it by the pound. Kids tend to be much more open-minded than we give them credit for when we don't impose our dislikes or opinions on them. At your next mealtime, try serving a veggie or fruit that you wouldn't expect your kid to be keen on and see what happens. Don't say anything or draw attention to it; let him discover it for himself. You just might be surprised by his response.

shopping: setting
yourself up for success

food shopping with the kids

Picture the scene: You're at your local supermarket. A child—likely your own—is screaming and crying in the cart or running down the aisles, grabbing things from the shelves, and there's no doubt in your mind that everyone in the store is looking at *you*.

We've all been there. For most moms, going to the supermarket with the kids in tow is about as much fun as a bikini wax. But I believe a lot of the agony stems from the experience we set up for our child in the supermarket: Do we just drag our kids along for the ride at the supermarket, creating a passive experience for them that's bound to make them succumb to every impulse or respond to any diversion, or do we make them active participants in the whole shopping process from the time we walk through the front doors? Allowing your child to be a collaborator has everything to do with how she views that weekly trip and is a good predictor of whether she spins

out of control or becomes fully engaged in helping you plan the week's menu, looking forward to the excitement of preparing it at home.

I'm not insinuating that you should permit your child to have free reign at the supermarket. Far from it. As with anything, you must set boundaries and predetermine the choices they have so that you can get the job done and ensure the overall experience is a positive one.

One of my favorite things to do with my kids is to let them choose a fruit or vegetable, talk about it, touch it, smell it, and decide with me what we're going to make with it when we get home. I highly recommend knowing beforehand what you're making and helping steer your child to that choice, but by involving them rather than just locating what's on your list and putting it in your cart with no explanation, you're giving your child the opportunity to buy into that meal from the very beginning.

An important note about choice: Sometimes too much of a good thing can be bad. If you give your kids unlimited and noncurated choices, it will overwhelm them, and it's just as bad as giving them no choice at all. Think ahead and limit your child's choices to two or three items. Your kids likely won't realize the boundaries you're setting up for them, and anyway, complete control is scary for kids—they don't want it as much as we think they do. For example, asking "Do you want broccoli or cauliflower" is far more comforting, manageable, and empowering for kids than rolling into the produce section and saying, "What should we cook today?" That would overwhelm my husband, let alone a three-year-old.

Here are a few tips that will make grocery shopping with your kids a lot more fun and easy:

- **Be prepared.** Have a detailed list of what you need to buy so that your shopping trip is focused. It's all too easy to get flustered while wandering the aisles aimlessly, trying to think of what you need and ferret out the best prices while your kids are peppering you with a million questions and requests.

- **Start small.** You don't need to give your child input into everything you put in the cart. Start small and build with every future trip. The first few times, let your child choose one thing that you'll make together for his lunch. For example, "Do you want pasta or a sandwich for school tomorrow?" You'll be surprised, but the excitement your child will derive from planning just one meal may get you through the entire shop!

- **Six of one . . .** If you have no preference between two brands of something you're buying or, say, two types of tomatoes, let your child decide which one you'll get. Either way, you get what you want, but the choice is all theirs!

- **Play a game.** Whenever you head down an aisle, know beforehand what you need to get there and have your child focused on finding that one particular thing. For example, if you need peanut butter and you know that to get to it you're going to have to make your way past the boxes of sugary cereal plastered with cartoon characters luring children like the Pied Piper, divert your child by saying something like, "Who can spot the peanut butter first, you or me?"

- **Helping hands.** Let your child help hand the cashier the foods as you check out. This is somewhat easier when your little one is still small enough to ride in the cart, but I find it to be quite empowering whatever their age, and it even helps kids work on their social skills as they interact with and get to know the people who work at your market.

- **Kids love teamwork.** Give older kids a copy of your shopping list. Bring a crayon and have them read what's needed to you and mark off the purchases as you find them.

moms and dads beware!

It would be nice to think that the supermarket is an ideal environment for trying all these tips, but make no doubt that there will be challenges placed for you at every turn. Once your kids are around two years old, their eyes will start spotting from a mile away the bright colors and cartoon characters found on kid-targeted food products (since stores strategically place all this stuff at eye level for kids, little ones don't have to work very hard to find it).

The one word most of us likely say to our children at the supermarket is "no." I bet if we counted how many times we tell our kids "no" in just one supermarket outing, we'd be shocked. And for our kids, why should they want to visit a place where "no" is the answer to almost every question? Well, don't be hard on yourself. It's not your fault. The supermarket is quite literally dripping with temptation for kids. While it's great living in a country of choice, the worst thing that most grocery stores do to parents is putting the bad stuff on their shelves in the first place. However, almost always, the crap vying for your kids' (and your) attention is shelved next to at least a few healthier choices, and directing kids to those choices is your job as a mom or dad.

I can't tell you how many times my son has begged me to buy him the cereal with the "happy gorilla" or the "funny bird" on the box. But instead of telling him, "No, you can't have that," I steer him toward two healthier choices and allow him to pick the one he prefers, turning a potentially negative experience into a positive one. Kids are sharp, so you need to be on your toes, but it yields results. More and more healthy foods are featuring appealing packaging these days, so try identifying something interesting for them on the label. It might not be as overt as a tiger in a kerchief, but you'll eventually grab their attention if you engage them. Kids can find something diverting in just about anything you involve them in—you just need to help lead the way.

shopping for high-quality food at the lowest prices possible

Our family loves going to the farmers' market every week to spend a leisurely morning outdoors together, but the benefits don't stop there. A recent study detailed in the *USA Today* article entitled "Fresh Food Diet Cuts Exposure to Chemical BPA" says it all in the headline. For many reasons, fresh is best. Besides the numerous physical and mental health benefits, I know that buying from our market supports local businesses, allows us to eat seasonally, and reduces our carbon footprint by not having a kitchen full of produce transported thousands of miles by way of planes, trains, and automobiles. Undeniably, there is no better way to eat any fresher or healthier than by shopping at farmers' markets— unless of course, you run a farm yourself.

If you have access to a farmers' market, use their products as the starting point when you construct your family's meals each week. I go to the farmers' market once a week to buy everything from eggs, to cheese, to bread, to meat, to fruits and vegetables. I then shop at groceries like Trader Joe's and our local supermarket to fill in the rest of my needs. After more than ten years of shopping regularly at farmers' markets, I've become skilled at feeding my family *and* saving money by doing things like buying slightly bruised tomatoes (80 percent below the regular price) to make sauces, soups, and salsas or getting better deals from frequenting a single vendor for fruits or vegetables. Most farmers and vendors give regular customers discounts, so along with making friends with some truly lovely people, it literally pays to get to know your farmers. And don't forget the free samples! I feed my kids breakfast every Sunday morning on the free samples alone! It's gotten to the point where I just let my two hungry kids loose and allow them to stuff themselves at a virtual walking kid buffet.

Some people criticize farmers' markets as being more expensive than your local supermarket. In most cases, they're not. Regardless, I look at the cost of eating well as a long-term investment that will ultimately save far more money down the road, and you have a chance to educate your children in the meantime, which will reap benefits for the rest of their lives. If you believe—as I do—that eating well significantly contributes to our well-being and reduces the likelihood of illness and disease, and when you factor in what the average family currently pays for medical care, spending a few cents more for a pound of organic apples at the farmers' market seems like a good deal to me in the long run. We spend plenty of time choosing the right gas for our cars, the best car seat for our kids—why wouldn't we invest in the most important asset of all, our bodies?

I realize that I have an unfair advantage living in Southern California, which has plenty of farmers' markets and seasonal produce in more variety than most places in the country. But when I lived in Kentucky and New York, I found *great* markets in both of those places, too. The Seasonal Ingredient Map on epicurious.com is a handy resource in discovering what's available in your area. Also, you can find your local farmers' markets, CSAs (Community Supported Agriculture), supermarkets, and restaurants that offer locally grown, raised, and produced food and at www.localharvest.org.

So try finding a few local markets in your area, plan a family outing, or just stop in yourself. I think you'll discover a great new alternative for feeding your family—if not a new way of life.

cooking healthy doesn't have to break the bank (or even come close!)

When you're attempting to save money in the kitchen, there are a few simple strategies to making nutritious meals that will cost you less than you would think possible. One of the easiest is to choose foods that are almost universally inexpensive, such as pasta, brown rice, eggs, and sweet potatoes, and whole grains like quinoa, millet, barley, and oats. Meat can be expensive, but if you treat it as a condiment rather than as the focus of your meal, a little bit will go a long way. I always keep a bag of frozen shrimp in my freezer; I can quickly defrost a few as needed, chop them up, and toss them with a little pasta, a veggie, and a light sauce. It's a fast, easy, delicious meal for less than two dollars a plate!

When I'm in the process of planning a meal, I think about two things: simplicity and balance.

I make sure everyone's plate has a protein, a carbohydrate, and a vegetable on it. A tight budget should not mean you have to sacrifice balance and nourishment, so focus on reasonably priced, nutritious items in each of these categories. For example, when you're thinking of serving a protein, a big piece of red meat is not required. Cheese, beans, eggs, quinoa, nut butters, tofu, and fish fillets such as cod and tilapia (which are less expensive than choices like tuna) are all excellent and affordable sources of protein.

And when it comes to fruits and vegetables, don't turn up your nose at frozen. As much as I advocate for fresh and recommend avoiding foods that come out of a can or box, fruits and vegetables that are flash frozen at their peak of freshness are usually more affordable and nutrient-rich than what you'll find in your local supermarket's produce section. Furthermore, you can keep a bag in your freezer for up to three months or more after opening it and portion out only what you need at each meal. That will stretch your food dollars a long way.

WEELICIOUS RECOMMENDS:
My Top Inexpensive and Nutritious Foods

Bananas	Frozen fruits and vegetables
Beans	Nut butters
Bread	Oats and oatmeal
Brown rice	Pasta (any shape you love)
Cheese	Potatoes
Couscous	Tofu
Eggs	Whole chicken

organic vs. non-organic and the "dirty dozen"

Years ago when I started really learning about what foods were best for my body and what "organic" meant, I had a ton of questions. Even though you may know the word "organic," it can be confusing to understand what you should be buying. Even though I find that most people are aware of the importance of buying organic, the specific reasons for doing so are not always as clear. Here are a few basic questions and answers on the subject that I find very helpful.

Q: What does organic mean?
A: *Food certified under United States Department of Agriculture regulations as organic must be produced without most synthetic pesticides and fertilizers. Antibiotics, growth hormones, and feed made from animal parts are also banned.*

Q: Aren't all natural foods organic?
A: *No, they're not. Foods may be free of artificial ingredients, or labeled "natural," but still grown by conventional methods. The term "organic" on the label means the food has been grown and processed according to strict guidelines, carefully documented, and certified.*

Q: Is buying organic worth the extra money?
A: *Research has yet to prove an adverse health effect from consuming the levels of the lowest pesticide load commonly found in food in the United States. But for the most vulnerable groups—children and pregnant women—going organic whenever possible*

for fruits and vegetables that carry the heaviest pesticide load makes sense. It might come down to your willingness to pay more to avoid supporting certain agricultural practices, such as antibiotic use in animals, which could promote resistant bacterial strains, or the use of growth hormones, which could prematurely wear down the animal.

Q: Why does organic food cost more?

A: Along with the simple rules of supply and demand, we must remember that prices fluctuate in our economy. Organic food prices are coming down, on the whole, and are expected to continue to drop as supply grows. Organic farming is also more labor-intensive than conventional farming, and usually takes place on a smaller scale than the so-called chemical agribusiness factory farms.

In the United States, conventional farming has often been subsidized by taxpayer funds through the government. Some believe that this keeps the price of conventional food artificially low, not reflecting the true cost of bringing food to market. Costs are externalized. Organic farmers do not receive these subsidies, and thus the shelf price may actually reflect a truer market cost.

The long-term price of conventional farming, in terms of the damage to our soil, water, farm workers' and children's health, and the loss of a family farm lifestyle, is great. We pay these costs when taxpayers fund environmental cleanup or health-care costs. This must be taken into account when measuring the costs and benefits of buying organic on our bodies.

Q: What if a label says pesticide-free, not organic—what's the difference?

A: Pesticide-free is just that, but you have to take it on faith. The producers aren't inspected to make sure they're doing what they say, while organic producers are inspected.

Q: Are there nutritional benefits to eating organic fruits and vegetables?

A: Children who eat organic foods have lower levels of pesticides in their bodies than those fed industrial foods.

A few studies show that organic foods are higher in minerals and some vitamins, but the increments are small. The real point of organics is better production methods so fewer chemicals will be polluting the soil and water.

For more information on organic, see the "Dirty Dozen" on page 23.

top ways to buy organic food for less money

- Shop at farmers' markets
- Buy a share in a Community Supported Agriculture (CSA) program
- Join a co-op
- Join a buying club
- Buy in bulk
- Buy fruits and vegetables big in-season
- Grow your own
- Freeze, can, dehydrate, or preserve fruits and vegetables that are becoming overripe

the "dirty dozen"

When I'm trying to decide where to spend my food dollars, I like to buy organic fruits and vegetables. Here's a list of the so-called Dirty Dozen, the twelve fruits and vegetables sold at your local supermarket that contain the *highest* pesticide residue. These are the fruits and vegetables you definitely want to buy organic.

Apples	Peaches
Celery	Pears
Cherries	Potatoes
Grapes (imported)	Spinach
Lettuce	Strawberries
Nectarines	Sweet bell peppers

Source: Environmental Working Group, www.ewg.org, and Food News, www.foodnews.org

other good foods to buy organic

Corn and soy products
Milk
Oats
Rice

seafood to buy wild

Shrimp
Salmon

Source: montereybayaquarium.org/seafoodwatch.aspx

the clean 15

These are the kinds of produce that are *lowest* in pesticides and are not as important to buy organic.

Asparagus	Mango
Avocado	Mushrooms
Cabbage	Onions
Cantaloupe	Pineapples
Corn (fresh)	Sweet peas
Eggplant	Sweet potatoes
Grapefruit	Watermelon
Kiwis	

Source: The Environmental Working Group's shopper's guide to pesticides in produce.

to learn more

USDA—ams.usda.gov

The website of the agricultural marketing service division of the USDA has the complete list of organic standards and a handy map of farmers' markets nationwide.

Local Harvest—localharvest.org

Head here for a directory of small farms and farmers' markets anywhere in the country. There's also an online store featuring products from family farms.

Organic Consumers Association—organicconsumers.org

Get information on the politics of organic and sustainable agriculture, and the latest organic news.

cooking: turning passive eaters into active ones

getting your kids involved in cooking

One of the biggest daily power struggles between kids and parents is *what* kids will eat and *when* they'll eat it. Kids aren't in charge of much (yes, they're kids and need schedules and boundaries, but think about how you'd feel if your life was managed to that degree), but the one thing they *can* control is the food that goes into their bodies. It's usually just one more thing being imposed upon them, but it's also the easiest thing for them to take charge of, simply by closing their mouths or pushing their food away.

Over the years I've heard and read many different theories on how to get kids to eat anything, let alone healthy foods: "Try sneaking broccoli into meatloaf," "Threaten to withhold their toys if they won't eat what you make them," "Keep cooking what you want and eventually they'll eat out of sheer hunger," and so on. It can become a kind of psychological warfare in which

parents and kids struggle to see who'll give in first. Try maintaining that dynamic over three meals and several snacks a day, and it quickly becomes an exhausting if not downright hopeless endeavor. Need it be so challenging to get kids to *want* to eat what's good for them? I say no. Look closely at the way a kid is wired, and the answers to many eating issues are simpler than we make them out to be.

I bet when you put your kids in a room full of toys, they behave much differently. No one is telling them what to play with or how to play. They can wander, observe, build, imagine, and play on their own clocks. Even the tiniest among us experiences the need for independence, and what kids have when they play, very simply, is choice. Choice is a powerful tool when it comes to food as well. The ultimate goal is to shift the act of eating for them from a *passive* experience (sitting kids at the table and putting a plate in front of them) to an *active* one (showing them where their food comes from, letting them help prepare their meals, asking them questions and answering theirs).

I got both of my kids involved in cooking when they were as young as six months old. I'd give Kenya a banana to peel, let Chloe put her little finger on the food processor button to help me puree, or place spoons in their hands to let them try to feed themselves. I believe that just these little steps helped them from their earliest contact with food to make firsthand connections, such as how an apple turns into applesauce or the fact that some fruit and vegetable skins can be eaten and some can't.

Cooking is fun. Cooking is art. Cooking is play. The more you can let kids take part in that fun, the more excited they'll become about the food that's going in their bodies. Even if you've never cooked before or get intimidated in the kitchen, making something basic with your child, like a smoothie or fresh fruit pop, will help you get an abundance of nutrients into your kids' tummies, and they'll have a blast making it with you at the same time.

starting day one

From the day they were first able to eat solids, I introduced my kids to a wide variety of fresh fruits, vegetables, and other nutritious foods. When I say "introduced," that didn't just entail preparing a rainbow of purees for them. Every great relationship starts with a "getting to know you" period, so that meant taking my kids to our local farmers' markets and grocery stores with me on a regular basis, allowing them to experience the produce themselves, and then letting them "cook" our purchases by giving them simple tasks to perform alongside me in the kitchen. For some people that may sound tedious or overwhelming, but it truly makes life easier—certainly in the long run. I found that once I let my kids get involved in what I was buying and preparing, it removed much of the pressure that I find many parents put on their kids to get them to eat. I never said to my kids, "You have (or need) to eat this." Rather, I acquainted them with new foods, let them taste

the goods beforehand whenever possible, gave them time to try things again, and from there, the most remarkable thing happened: They formed their own opinions!

Are my kids gourmets? No way! Will they eat just about anything I make for them? Absolutely. That's not because I think they have extraordinary palates or that they're geniuses (well, I'm their mother—of course I think they're geniuses, but that's not why they eat so well). I realize that by making my kids a part of the whole process, they've gotten to form their *own* attitudes about the food they put into their bodies.

Here are some age-appropriate tasks your kids can be doing in the kitchen, to inspire you:

infants

From the first day your baby is able to eat food (generally around six months; see page 47, but consult your pediatrician), it's important to get him involved. Up to this age, babies have been naturally passive eaters, so they'll likely welcome the opportunity to become active and part of what you do. Start small by allowing him to hold his own spoon while you feed him with another. When your baby is able to sit in a high chair, it's the perfect time to give her a shatterproof bowl and small whisk or wooden spoon so she can imitate some of your moves in the kitchen. When it comes to involving your child, you'll find you can't start too young. The rich sensory and culinary experience a baby receives when she gets to see, smell, and taste through play is an essential part of kids getting excited about food.

- **Familiarity breeds comfort.** Meals should repeat the same rituals so that your baby gets accustomed to the feeding experience: Get in the high chair, wash hands with a damp towel, put on a bib, and let the fun begin.

- **It's mine!** Help your baby be part of the feeding process by giving him his own spoon, cup, or bowl to play with during the meal.

- **Don't give up!** At mealtime, start with the foods your baby struggles with most. When little ones are hungry they're more likely to eat the foods they normally refuse, so it's a good time to let them retry things.

- **"Sleeping Beauty" is a fairy tale.** Many parents begin feeding their babies solids too young because they think it will help them sleep through the night. There's no scientific proof to support this theory.

- **Feeding is a bonding experience.** Ignore your phone and turn off the TV to help focus you both on the eating process and allow for priceless one-on-one time.

- **Let me try!** Soon after your baby has mastered eating purees, she will likely begin trying to reach for the food on *your* plate. This is a good sign that she's ready to start trying solids. Allow her to begin feeding herself small pieces of food, and always make sure you're supervising and encouraging when needed.

- "You say potato..." When you're feeding your baby, say what he is eating out loud before each bite so he learns to identify different foods by name. This exercise will help baby learn what it is he wants to eat, and begin to teach him to communicate it to you in the future.

- Variety is the *spice* of life. Herbs and spices add a ton of dimension to even the most simple of foods, eliminating the need for salt (which is unnecessary for babies learning the true tastes of food). You can use fresh or dried, but keep in mind that dried herbs and spices are more concentrated and so less is required to flavor a dish. Start by adding just a pinch of the spice or herb to the puree; you don't want to overpower the food itself. Some perfect pairings: sweet potato and cinnamon; black beans and cilantro; butternut squash and nutmeg; peas and fresh mint; cauliflower and paprika; pears and ginger; carrots and cumin.

- Sometimes *no* really means *no.* Never force your baby to eat. Babies self-regulate naturally, and a healthy baby generally will stop eating when full.

- Keep it fun! Sing songs, make silly faces, or play other fun games when you think your baby's losing steam. This will keep her mentally engaged and focused on the task at hand.

preschoolers (two to five years old)

When your child is two years old or more, the real fun begins. Because her motor skills are much stronger, your child is actually able to participate in the cooking process. Toddlers' attention spans can be short, but their eagerness to control situations is great. Giving them even the tiniest of jobs or tasks can be totally empowering. Kids love to copy and emulate their parents, so if they see that you enjoy cooking, very likely they will too. Your child may have already mastered peeling bananas or pressing the "start" button on a blender or food processor, which lets him watch how food can change form, and now is ready for some more responsibilities. Here's a list of some activities that are generally safe for this age, educational, and make cooking loads of fun:

- Kneading, rolling, twisting, or crimping dough when making pizza, breadsticks, or calzones is fun, utilizes kids' upper arm strength, and works on their dexterity. These techniques can be a unique sensory experience, allowing them to manipulate the food with their hands, which most kids love. Explaining to them the steps involved from start to finish helps teach kids to follow instructions.

- Turning on the tap: I don't know many kids who don't like turning on a faucet when given the chance, so pull up a chair or stool (or hold them up to the sink) to get some water for a recipe or to wash their hands before cooking.

- Pouring liquid ingredients into a bowl will get him excited and allow him to feel involved in the cooking process (this is always one of my son's favorite jobs in the kitchen).

- Sifting dry ingredients into a bowl is visually interesting (you can pretend that it's like snow falling) and educational (explain to your child that you combine the dry ingredients before adding them to the liquids so that they are distributed evenly).

- Mashing potatoes or other veggies gets kids to use their muscles and teaches them how manipulating food transforms it into another shape and texture. And it's fun!

- Letting your kids use a wooden knife (without a real blade) to try cutting foods (another one of my son's favorite activities when he was around three years old) makes them feel like they're doing a real grown-up job.

- Washing fruits or vegetables in a big bowl of water and then placing them on a towel to dry shows kids the importance of cleaning produce (and teaches them to conserve water).

- Cutting shapes out of sandwiches with cookie cutters gives them ownership over the food they'll be eating—especially if they get to choose their favorite cutter.

- Shaking jars of dried herbs or spices into a pot or learning how to measure them out with a spoon is a great way to teach children the importance of quantities and balancing flavors in a recipe.

- Whisking ingredients in a bowl is one of the most basic, kid-friendly cooking chores and one of the most exciting tasks for this age group.

- Adding a pinch of salt (with their first finger and thumb, which I call their pinching fingers) to a recipe is a fun one—it's hands down my son's favorite kitchen activity.

- Being "in charge" of the timer to tell you when things are finished cooking. Let your child hold or be responsible for listening for the timer to go off. This helps kids develop a sense of time and responsibility.

- Being "in charge" of passing you ingredients gives kids purpose and makes them feel responsible while giving them a subtle education in cooking.

- Sprinkling cheese into a bowl of pasta (if it's not too hot) and helping to toss it and incorporate the ingredients is a safe and fun activity at this age.

- Having your little one walk her own plate to the sink so you can rinse it teaches her to be responsible.

Most important, talk with your child as you're cooking! The more you help kids to understand what you're doing during food preparation—*why* you're cutting, stirring, chopping, and so on—the more you'll engage them and get them excited about the food they're making for themselves to eat!

school-age kids (six-plus)

When kids are age six and up, they can start getting even more immersed in cooking. Kids this age are learning to read and will be better at following directions, so in addition to learning and having fun, they can be of great assistance to you. This is also a great age to give children a voice in the cooking process by asking them for their opinion about ingredients that could be added to a dish. That being said, kids this age may believe their ability is greater than it really is, so always keep an eye out and continue to safeguard knives or other objects that may be just beyond their skill set. They'll enjoy activities like these:

- Learning to use hand-powered kitchen tools such as can openers and juicers.

- Operating the hand mixer (with your supervision) to stir batter or beat eggs so they can see how the mixture increases in volume.

- Using the toaster and preparing their own sandwiches for school lunch. Remember, they're more likely to eat what they make themselves.

- Peeling fruits and vegetables for you to chop up.

- Reading recipes with your assistance. They'll learn the importance of following directions from beginning to end.

- Taking on specific tasks within a recipe. They'll understand how parts come together to create a whole.

- "Shopping" in the refrigerator or pantry for foods you'll be using for a given recipe. Explain what each one is used for in the recipe before you start cooking.

- Portioning out doughs and other mixtures, such as dividing batter into muffin cups, forming equal-size meatballs, and scooping cookie dough onto a cookie sheet.

- Separating egg yolks from whites. This takes some skill and practice, but it soon becomes one of the more exciting kitchen activities for children. Be patient with this one, and have extra eggs on hand!

- Arranging food on plates or platters for serving. The "oohs" and "ahhs" they receive from the family can be truly gratifying for kids this age and magnify the pride they take in their work.

- Setting the table and cleaning up after the meal are important parts of the process as well. Make it fun!

the work pays off!

The effort involved in getting kids to eat healthy food pays dividends, in my experience. One Halloween—the dreaded death knell day for kids and healthy eating—two-and-a-half-year-old Kenya was having a meltdown right before it was time for him to go to bed. He was in my husband's arms, squirming for freedom and reaching toward his bag of trick-or-treat candy, which was sitting on the kitchen counter. (Yes, candy. I'm obviously not big on candy, but I believe in moderation, and kids deserve to enjoy a piece of candy every once in a while.) My husband and I looked at each other. *Oh no*, we both thought, *all our hard work has been ruined by this holiday!* My husband walked Kenya closer to the counter. His plan (he told me later) was to let Kenya carry the bag to his room to get him upstairs quietly. Then he would dispose of the evil bag of sweets after Kenya went to bed. However, as they got to the counter, Kenya reached down—his hand moving past the Halloween candy and just behind it—to where a bowl of cherry tomatoes was sitting, obscured from my husband's and my view. Kenya took a handful of tomatoes, immediately became calm, and happily went up to bed. We went from fear to enormous pride in a matter of seconds. Our efforts at shaping his culinary cravings had succeeded!

you're not a short-order cook: how not to be a slave to your kids in the kitchen

How often at mealtime have you felt like the cook in the kitchen of your local diner, getting different food orders shouted at you as you race the clock to make the dinner rush? I find it incredible how many of us moms succumb to this practice of making a different meal for each member of our family. One of my major goals is to help parents put a stop to short-order cook syndrome. There's simply no reason that everyone in your house can't enjoy the same basic meal—even Mom and Dad. It's easy, cost-effective, and a great way to bring the whole family together.

- **The magic of three-in-ones.** Build your weekly menus from your family's favorite foods. I'm a big fan of three-in-one recipes, which help me do more with less. For example, my family loves rice, so on Sundays I make a big pot of brown rice, and over the next three days I'll turn it into different rice-based dishes, such as Shrimp "Fried" Rice (page 188) on Monday, Miso Marinated Fish (page 194) on rice on Tuesday, and Brown Rice and Veggie Casserole (page 162) on Wednesday.

- **One for all; no one too small.** If you make Slow-Cooker Lentil Veggie Stew (page 101), you can puree it for your little one while the rest of your family eats it over rice. Same for many of the dishes you'll find in this book, which can be chopped up or pureed to feed your baby or toddler or made to be the appropriate texture for different age groups.

- **Freedom of choice.** Whenever you can give your child a choice, it helps. I'm not talking about which entrée they want, but if you have two vegetables in your fridge or freezer, offering, "Do you want broccoli or edamame on the side?" helps them feel like they have some say in what they're about to eat.

- **Take turns!** This works better with older kids, but once a week, allow kids to "plan" the menu by offering to make one of their favorite things. Come mealtime, they know that everyone in the family is eating what *they* picked. If you're someone who likes to plan ahead, it can be a fun and effective mealtime strategy.

your basic kitchen gear

Most of what you need is already in your kitchen, but here are some of my favorite kitchen devices and utensils.

- **Mini-prep food processor** (4 cups)—an essential tool for making homemade baby food. It's also great for small-batch pureeing (like making pesto) and for jobs that entail chopping (if you're not great with a knife).

- **Food processor.** Cuisinart is the mack daddy of food processors. It holds up to 9 cups, so you can make big batches of everything from hummus to pureed soups to dough. It's also genius for chopping and shredding.

- **Silicone steamer insert** to fit into most pots is great for steaming and cooking fruits and vegetables prior to pureeing. It's also a *quiet* kitchen toy that your baby can play with while you're cooking!

- Pyrex, Kinetic, or Frigoverre **glass containers** for storing food. Plastic can leech harmful chemicals into your food and is bad for the environment. I prefer these glass containers, which last forever and clean up easily in the dishwasher.

- Good **chef's** and **paring knives.** I can't live without them. Victorinox makes an amazing inexpensive chef's knife. Wüsthof makes great knives of every type, but they can be pricey. When it comes to knives, the great chef Jacques Pépin offered my favorite piece of advice when asked what the best knife is: "A sharp one."

- **Ice pop molds** (preferably BPA free). Kids love ice pops, and there are plenty of healthy ones you can make that they'll love eating and you'll love because they supply needed vitamins and nutrients.

- **Ice cube tray** or **baby cubes** like the ones from Wean Green or OXO for freezing and storing baby food purees.

- **High-heat silicone spatulas** in assorted sizes are some of the most indispensable tools in the kitchen. I use them constantly for everything from stirring to getting every last bit of mustard or jelly out of a jar. A lifesaver.

- By placing a **Silpat** on a cookie sheet, you can bake the most delicious cookies—perfect every time—and it makes cleanup so much easier. They also last forever.

- **Mini muffin tins** are obviously great for making muffins and cupcakes, but I also use them to make meatloaf and other bite-size meals for the kids, since they love anything with handheld appeal!

- A **slow cooker** will completely change a busy mom's world. Cook entire meals in a fraction of the time required by conventional cooking. Just dump in all of your ingredients and let your slow cooker do the rest of the work!

- From omelets to quesadillas, an inexpensive **cast-iron pan** cooks everything to perfection with limited added fat.

- Whether you're shredding sweet potatoes or carrots for muffins, grating potatoes for hash browns, or grating cheese for quesadillas, a **grater** will make your life much easier. Get a durable one—I've had the same one for more than twenty years!

- Every kitchen should have a few dishwasher-safe **cutting boards.**

- I can't tell you how many meals I've ruined by forgetting to set a **timer.** Essential!

- I use **kitchen shears** for everything from cutting herbs to removing the fat from chicken.

They're dishwasher safe, which I love, and it's great to have a pair of scissors in the kitchen so I don't have to search around every time I need one.

- An assortment of Wilton **nonstick baking pans** for making everything from breads to cakes.

- When turning meat and veggies on the grill or in the oven, a good set of **tongs** will prevent many a burned finger. Take it from me—I have the scars to prove that I should have invested in a pair much earlier than I did.

- The **blender** seems to never stop whirling in our house, making smoothies, ice pops, soups, and when my kids were tiny, baby food purees.

- A few inexpensive **wooden spoons** are invaluable for everything from stirring sauce to stir-fries to using with pots and pans to make a drum set!

- Speaking of **pots and pans,** dust off that set you got for your wedding and put them to good use. They also make great instruments for keeping babies busy while you're cooking!

- An assortment of **mixing bowls** always comes in handy to help you with both small and big jobs, from stirring to whisking to making guacamole or storing leftovers.

- From preparing muffins to cupcakes to pancake batter, a **whisk** is a kitchen must-have and safe tool for *everyone* to use in the kitchen.

- Where's your grandmother's **pie plate**? Use it for baking pies and even baked pasta dishes.

- If there's one safe cooking tool that all kids love to use, it's a **rolling pin.**

- Pasta always needs to be drained and fruits and veggies need to be washed, so you'll need a good metal **strainer.**

- From cooling cookies on the counter to making super-healthy foods that are crisp on the outside and tender on the inside, a **cooling rack** ensures you aren't stuck with soggy food!

- **Cookie cutters**: There's nothing more fun than turning food into different shapes.

- A **Sharpie marker** and **painter's tape**: If you're like me and can't remember when you refrigerated or froze a particular food, put a piece of painter's tape on the container and write the date it was prepared on it.

- And don't forget **measuring cups and spoons.** A must-have for most recipes.

weelicious cooking staples

When it comes to mealtime, the best way to make mom's life easy in the kitchen is keeping a stocked pantry full of foods that are nutritious and simple to prepare, and have a long shelf life. Here are a few of our family's favorites.

grains, flours, and cereals

- Brown rice (short- and long-grain)
- Couscous
- Flax seeds
- Nature's Path Organic Heritage Flakes cereal
- Oatmeal or rice cereal
- Quaker old-fashioned oats or McCann's steel-cut oats
- Pasta (in a variety of shapes and flavors)
- Quinoa
- Wheat germ
- Whole wheat and/or white flour (King Arthur brand)

refrigerated items

- Almond butter (I prefer Trader Joe's or Barney Butter brands) and peanut butter
- Bragg Liquid Aminos
- Cheddar and mozzarella cheese
- Organic cow's milk. I buy only organic milk because it has a longer shelf life and is free of the antibiotics and rBGH hormone that factory farms give their cows to increase their milk production. (rBGH is banned by the European Union, Australia, Canada, and other countries because of its health risks for humans.)
- Rice or almond milk (Trader Joe's brand is Kenya's and Daddy's milk preferences)
- Organic eggs
- Parmesan cheese (whole or grated)
- Toasted sesame oil
- Firm and silken tofu
- Unsalted organic butter
- Veganaise (vegan mayonnaise; I'm not a vegan, but Veganaise is lower in fat than most mayos and contains no hydrogenated or partially hydrogenated fat and no trans fats.)
- Greek yogurt (0% Fage or Oikos brands)
- Organic ketchup (Muir Glen brand)

freezer items

While my love of farmers' markets and fresh produce abounds, frozen foods have many advantages. They obviously keep a long time; they're very economical, as you can use just what you need; and their nutrient content is as rich as fresh, as most frozen fruits and vegetables are frozen when they are just picked. Plus, you can defy Mother Nature. For example, in January, when strawberries aren't in season but you still want to make something with them, a bag of frozen can make it feel like summertime. You can always find the following in my freezer.

- Broccoli florets
- Corn

- Edamame
- Green beans
- Mango
- Mixed berries
- Okra (cut)
- Peas
- Wild shrimp (uncooked)
- Strawberries

fresh produce

- Apples
- Avocados
- Bananas
- Carrots
- Celery
- Cherry tomatoes
- Fresh herbs (basil, thyme, parsley, and cilantro are my staples)
- Garlic
- Ginger
- Kale
- Lemons
- Onions
- Oranges
- Persian cucumbers
- Sweet potatoes
- Russet and fingerling potatoes

in the pantry

- Agave nectar (Madhava brand, dark or light)
- Baking powder
- Baking soda
- Beans (dried or canned)
- Bread crumbs or panko
- Brown rice syrup (Lundberg brand)
- Canned tomatoes (Muir Glen brand)
- Canola or vegetable oil
- Cinnamon
- Cocoa powder (Hershey's)
- Coconut milk
- Cumin
- Curry powder
- Dried apricots and cherries
- Honey (for babies over one year)
- Olive oil
- Organic vegetable oil spray (Spectrum brand)
- Raisins
- Rice cakes (Suzie's brand)
- Salt-free seasoning (Vegit brand)
- Sea salt or kosher salt (for kids over 18 months)
- Sorghum molasses
- Vanilla extract

eating: secrets revealed!

giving kids some choice

After talking over the years with thousands of mothers and listening to their cooking stories, I've concluded that most of us have all assumed one, if not all, of the following roles to get our kids to eat better:

The Dictator: "You have to eat this now!"
The Beggar: *"Please.* Just try it. You'll like it!"
The Compromiser: "Fine, just have two bites and you can be done."
The Negotiator: "If you eat your spinach you can have a cookie!"

Or worse, as mentioned before:

The Sneaker/Deceiver: "It's a chocolate brownie [that I secretly made with carrots and spinach]!"

While these timeworn tactics are easy to adopt when our kids refuse to eat what we make for them, it's important to realize how important choice is for a child who has very little control over her own life.

I find choice to be the number one most important rule in getting kids excited about the foods they should be eating. Given the chance, my children can be incredibly challenging to deal with when it comes to food. But as I said earlier, whenever I introduce a little bit of choice into the equation, you would be amazed at how quickly they make the better decision for themselves (and most times it's exactly what I intended for them to eat).

Again, it all comes down to treating mealtime as an active rather than a passive experience for kids. It applies to all of us. If whenever it was time for you to eat, you were served a plate of food you had no hand in choosing, making, or preparing, you'd probably get a little frustrated too. Imagine now if that was your mealtime experience every day, because that's what it's like for most kids. On the other hand, think of how enjoyable eating is when you have a voice in the matter. Again, I'm not suggesting you give your kids free reign—you have to control their choices, and that is fairly easy to do—but being heard matters to everyone, no matter what their age.

a little goes a long way

Even on those busy nights when I've already decided what we're going to be eating, I give the kids a little say. Inclusive dialogue such as, "Would you prefer the red plate or the blue plate?" or "Do you want the black beans *on* your rice or *next to* your rice?" treats little ones with respect and makes it more likely for them to buy into the meal. Alternately, when you innocently or arbitrarily put the beans on their rice, you're introducing the element of surprise into the mix. Kids like surprise when it comes to presents—not food. A sense of control and familiarity are crucial for them, and if your "surprise" doesn't go over well ("I wanted my beans *next* to my rice!"), you've lost a battle that could have easily been won. Kids being kids, they may ask you for two separate plates, each positioned in an unusual way, with beans on one and rice on the other. I say give in. Sure, it requires washing an extra plate or two and a minimal amount of extra effort, but at the end of the day, if your kids are eating well, does it matter?

making food fun

If something's perceived as fun, kids will want to do it. So when you start approaching cooking and eating as art, or even a game, then all of a sudden it becomes a lot more intriguing. The more interactive food is for kids—from the time you grow it in your garden or purchase it at the store until the time you eat it—the more they will embrace the process, enjoy it, and treat food as something they want to be a part of.

Here are a few of my favorite tips for making food more of a fun experience.

- Serve raw or steamed veggies with a dip. Two of my kids' favorites are Ranch Dip (page 113) and Ricotta Veggie Dip (page 114).

- Let kids sprinkle a salt-free seasoning or even a few drops of something like Bragg Liquid Aminos (a natural amino acid you can buy at most groceries that tastes just like soy sauce). This may not seem like a big deal, but kids tend to enjoy most anything that gives them a hand in making something or "personalizing" it. I've seen plain steamed vegetables that might well have sat there untouched disappear off my kids' plates after strategically putting out a shaker of salt-free seasoning.

- Let kids cut their food (such as sandwiches, polenta, and certain fruits and veggies) into fun shapes using cookie cutters. You'd be surprised at how much a car- or dog-shaped cookie cutter can enhance the appeal of a particular food for a kid.

- Similarly, if your child resists a certain food, try cutting it into different shapes or sizes. Make sure the pieces are bite size. Many children will spit food out if the pieces are too large—it's about size, not the food itself. The sensation of food that's too big can be very uncomfortable for a child, and she may not have the vocabulary to communicate that to you.

- Presentation is key. Serving food in small cups, on colorful plates, with a straw, or even in unusual containers like brightly colored silicone muffin cups make mealtime special and add an element of whimsy.

- Once in a while, encourage your child to eat with her fingers. It's good for fine motor skills and makes eating a lot more stimulating.

the family that eats together . . .

When you really stop and think about it, how often does your whole family get to sit together and enjoy a meal?

Among the many benefits it provides kids, eating together as a family inspires kids to become better eaters. Countless studies have shown that families who eat together have better overall nutrition than families who do not. In addition, kids who eat with their families statistically do better in school, have a greater sense of family, and have improved language development.

In this busy world where working parents often can't make it to the dinner table on time, it's important to try to set aside at least one or two nights a week to eat and cook together as a family. When I was growing up, our big family Sunday night dinner taught me the pleasures of eating and the importance of sharing a meal with loved ones, and encouraged me to try foods I probably wouldn't have had I not witnessed the examples of those sitting next to me. Times like the ones I spent perched next to my grandfather, helping him pop the ends off of sugar snap peas and eating them one after the other, are vivid memories I will carry with me forever.

Now that I have my own kids, my husband and I have started our own tradition of preparing and eating dinner every Sunday night as a family. In the morning, we all head out to our local farmers' market, decide together what we're going to make for dinner that night, and pick out everything as a team. By getting the kids involved in every step, from the selecting of produce to the cooking, tasting, and the eventual eating, we witness firsthand our children's desire to emulate Mommy and Daddy. Our kids clearly love the social experience of dining together, too. When Kenya was three, he invented a game called Happy and Sad which we now all—even three-year-old Chloe—take part in at every family meal. We go around the table and each of us says what made us happy and sad that day. You'd be surprised by how much more I've learned about my kids, my husband, and even myself by sharing those things with each other. Our simple Sunday meal tradition prompted Kenya's game and a great new sense of family life that we look forward to every time we all sit down to the table.

PART 2
RECIPES

baby purees

brown rice cereal

Like a lot of moms, I started feeding my kids brown rice cereal when they were six months old. The baby food companies perform some of their most impressive marketing when it comes to this tried-and-true first food, because while I bought it by the boxful, it never occurred to me that I could try making it at home. Guess what? All you need is a blender and some brown rice. It's truly *the* easiest thing you can make your baby.

Packed with iron, magnesium, and other vitamins and minerals, brown rice cereal makes a perfect first food. No more nutritionally stripped white rice cereal or spending way too much money on pretty packaging and advertising. Make it on your own and you'll have a simple food that your baby will love!

4 to 6 servings

½ cup organic short-grain brown rice

1. Place the rice in a spice grinder or blender and grind for 45 seconds to 1 minute, until finely ground. (This dry cereal keeps well in the refrigerator or a cool, dark place.)

2. To make 1 serving for a 4- to 6-month-old baby, in a small saucepan over medium-low heat, bring ½ cup water to a boil and sprinkle in 2 tablespoons of the ground rice. Whisk continuously for 30 seconds and then occasionally for 4 to 5 minutes, until the mixture is thick and creamy, to prevent lumps. Serve as is or with one of these additions: breast milk, formula, molasses, mashed banana, rice milk or almond milk, applesauce, baby food puree.

ANN: I've made the brown rice cereal for my eight-month-old many times and he gobbles it up! He likes it so much better than the boxed stuff. It's easy to make, too.

butternut squash puree

12 to 20 servings,
depending on the
size of the squash

1 butternut squash

Kenya is addicted to butternut squash. It was one of the very first purees I fed him, and I certainly ate a lot of it myself when I was pregnant, so maybe he was conditioned to love it. Smooth, creamy, sweet, easy for baby to get down, and totally wholesome, butternut squash is also great to keep on hand to mix into other baby purees to help enhance taste and texture.

This simple puree is a must for all beginning eaters. Loaded with beta-carotene, fiber, and vitamin C, it's mighty tasty and has a lot of nutritional punch.

1. Preheat the oven to 350°F and line a baking sheet with foil (for easier cleanup).

REFRIGERATING AND FREEZING PUREES

Purees will keep for up to 3 days in the refrigerator or for 2 to 3 months in the freezer.

2. Cut the squash in half from top to bottom and scrape out the seeds.

3. Place the squash halves cut side down on the baking sheet.

4. Bake for 45 minutes, or until the squash yields easily to a fork. Set the squash aside to cool for several minutes.

5. With a spoon, scrape out the soft pulp into a food processor and puree until smooth.

6. Cool before serving.

sweet potato–coconut puree

In my quest to find new ingredients that will tempt babies' taste buds, I realized that I had never tried using coconut milk in my purees. Sweet and creamy, it adds body and depth to this puree. Add a touch of cinnamon: yummy delicious.

1. Preheat the oven to 400°F.

2. Poke several holes in the sweet potatoes with a fork and place them on a piece of foil on a baking sheet (the foil will keep your baking sheet clean).

3. Bake the sweet potatoes for 1 hour, or until tender. Set them aside to cool.

4. When the sweet potatoes are cool to the touch, peel off the skin. Add the flesh to a food processor with the coconut milk and cinnamon. Puree until smooth.

5. Cool before serving.

TIP: *When you're choosing sweet potatoes (sometimes referred to as yams), look for those that are dark orange in color because they'll be a lot sweeter.*

12 servings

2 medium sweet potatoes, washed

⅓ cup canned coconut milk (light or full-fat is fine)

1 teaspoon ground cinnamon

SHANNON: I made this puree countless times for my girls when they were starting solids—and still do now that they're toddlers! The creamy, sweet blend of flavors makes it perfectly suited for babies, toddlers, and grown-ups! Yummy!

"eat your greens" puree

8 to 10 servings

½ cup peeled and cubed sweet potato

½ cup chopped baby carrots

½ cup chopped green beans (ends removed)

½ cup broccoli florets

½ cup peas (fresh or frozen)

Back before I started weelicious, when I first began cooking for my son, my mom's refrain, "Eat your greens!" echoed in my head whenever I was in the kitchen. Well, there I was, the new parent, trying to get my son to eat his greens. He actually was amazing about it, and I realize now that feeding him purees like this one helped cultivate the great palate he has now.

The mix of vegetables in this puree is colorful and bursting with vitamins and minerals. I added the carrots and sweet potatoes to give it a little more body and sweetness. Even a baby who turns his or her nose up at greens will love this mix—it's really yummy.

1. Place the sweet potato and carrots in a steamer pot over boiling water, cover, and cook for 4 minutes.

2. Add the remaining ingredients and steam for another 3 minutes, or until fork-tender.

3. Place the steamed vegetables in a food processor and puree.

4. Cool before serving.

BECCA: I used your recipes and made most of my baby food. I'm very proud to say my four-year-old daughter says quite often, "More broccoli, please."

FRANKI: The "Eat Your Greens" Puree was a staple for us while my daughter was eating purees. I loved how it was packed with super-nutritious veggies—it's a great start for a baby's diet. It was such a wonderful feeling to see my little one gobbling it up! Almost four years later and we're still huge weelicious fans.

TARA: The "Eat Your Greens" Puree has been a surprising hit with my little gaffer, who pretty much hates anything out of a jar.

roast pear and banana puree

6 servings

2 bananas, peeled and cut into 1-inch pieces

2 pears, peeled, cored, and cut into wedges

When Chloe started eating solids, I hadn't made purees for a long time—since Kenya was a baby, in fact—so I got excited to start working on a whole new set of baby food recipes. There's nothing wrong with pureeing ripe pears and bananas together, but when you roast them first it intensifies the flavors and texture even more. Pears and bananas are a good source of fiber, so they'll help to get things moving when your little one gets stopped up.

The only hard part about this puree for me is trying to keep it away from everyone else in our family! It's so yummy, you'll want to serve it on top of yogurt or spread on a bagel with almond butter.

1. Preheat the oven to 400°F and line a baking sheet with parchment paper or a Silpat.

2. Place the bananas and pears on the baking sheet and roast for 25 minutes, or until the pears are tender.

3. Place the fruit and any juices in a food processor and puree until smooth.

4. Cool before serving.

JEN: Absolutely delicious! I made this yesterday and my eight-month-old loved it. So did everyone else in the family—even Grandpa.

COURTNEY: Just made my husband try a sample of this, and he asked me to make him some to pack in his lunch for work. Hopefully my babies like it just as much as we do!

TIFFANY: This was amazing—my nine-month-old literally licked the bowl clean.

mint and pea puree

Peas seem like a perfect baby food—and they are—but pureed on their own they can take on a funny texture that some babies may struggle with. I remember both of my kids spitting out pea puree the first few times they tried it. I found that by mixing the peas with some sweet banana and fresh mint, the texture and taste became more appealing to them. It turned a simple baby food puree into something quite special.

Place all the ingredients in a food processor and puree.

8 servings

1 cup frozen peas, defrosted

1 banana

1 tablespoon chopped fresh mint

1 tablespoon rice milk, almond milk, or water

KATEE: Honestly, starting to make my daughter's food with fresh ingredients completely changed everything. She couldn't stand the premade, overcooked, tasteless jarred foods I bought in the store. I was so worried that I'd have a picky eater on my hands, but as it turned out, she just wanted good stuff. She eats anything I put in front of her now.

lentil vegetable puree

8 servings

2 teaspoons olive oil

2 tablespoons chopped carrot

2 tablespoons chopped celery

2 tablespoons chopped yellow onion

½ cup brown, green, or red lentils

½ cup chopped kale

¼ teaspoon garlic powder

¼ teaspoon dried thyme

Once your baby gets the hang of eating a variety of single food purees, it's fun to kick it up and start mixing a variety of veggies that work really well together. The lentils in this recipe are rich in protein and act as a creamy binder for all the other ingredients. Give your baby her own spoon and bowl of this delicious puree and let the culinary adventure (and mess) begin!

1. Heat the oil in a small saucepan over medium heat. Add the carrot, celery, and onion and sauté for 4 minutes, or until tender.

2. Add 1¼ cups water and the remaining ingredients and bring to a boil. Reduce to a simmer, cover, and cook for 45 minutes, or until the lentils are tender.

3. Transfer the mixture to a food processor and puree until smooth.

4. Cool before serving.

roast ginger-apple puree

I often refer to myself as a lazy cook. Sure, I'm busy and don't want to spend any more time in the kitchen than I have to, but for me it's especially important to avoid doing extra dishes. Aside from my genuine love of simple cooking, that's why I focus on straightforward recipes.

When my kids were babies, I loved making them this puree because it required no cleanup. All the ingredients go onto a piece of parchment paper that you just throw away (in the recycling bin, of course) after cooking, and with just a quick pulse in the easy-to-rinse food processor, you have a caramel-y apple ginger puree that's heaven for your brand-new eater. Never let anyone tell you that laziness isn't a virtue.

1. Preheat the oven to 400°F.

2. Place a 1-foot-square piece of parchment paper on a flat surface and fold it in half like a book.

3. Place all the ingredients on one side of the fold, fold over the other side, and starting at one end of the parchment, fold the edges of the paper over several times. Work your way around until you've created an airtight packet.

4. Place the packet on a baking sheet and bake for 20 minutes.

5. Cut the top open, taking care to avoid the steam in the packet, and place the baked apple and accumulated juices in a food processor. Puree until smooth.

6. Cool before serving.

6 servings

2 Gala, Pink Lady, Fuji, or other sweet apples, peeled, cored, and cut into 2-inch cubes (ripe pears work as well)

⅛ teaspoon ground cinnamon

⅛ teaspoon grated fresh ginger

the teething cookie

12 cookies

1 egg yolk, beaten

2 tablespoons
vegetable or canola oil

2 tablespoons
blackstrap molasses

1 teaspoon pure vanilla
extract

1 tablespoon milk
(cow's, rice, or soy)

¾ cup whole wheat
flour, plus 1 tablespoon
for rolling

1 tablespoon soy flour

1 tablespoon wheat
germ

Is your baby cutting teeth and in need for something special to chew on? These teething cookies are a breeze to make and a delicious treat your baby will love. I love that there's no sugar in them and they're packed with healthy nutrients.

I couldn't resist the picture below. It was the first time Kenya tried *The Teething Cookie*, and he devoured it. He had so much fun holding it, eating it, sucking on it, and rubbing it on his gums. I used to give him and Chloe one every night after dinner when they were babies. It was a great treat before bedtime.

1. Preheat the oven to 350°F and lay a piece of parchment paper or a Silpat on a baking sheet.

2. Place the egg yolk, oil, molasses, vanilla, and milk in a food processor and pulse to combine.

3. Whisk the ¾ cup whole wheat flour, the soy flour, and wheat germ in a separate bowl, then add them to the wet ingredients. Pulse until the mixture forms a ball.

4. Sprinkle the remaining 1 tablespoon whole wheat flour on a clean surface and shape the dough into a 6 x 6-inch, ½-inch-thick square.

5. With a knife, cut the dough into 1-inch-wide logs and place them on the baking sheet.

6. Bake the cookies for 10 minutes, or until firm. Cool them on the baking sheet or on a wire rack before serving.

STORAGE: *The cookies may be stored in an airtight container at room temperature for 2 days or in the refrigerator for 1 week.*

NOTE: *These cookies are for babies eight months and older, and you definitely need to supervise your baby to avoid choking.*

CASEY: When my son was teething we made *The* Teething Cookie, and he *loved* them! As he got teeth fairly young, he hadn't had a lot of solid foods, but these were perfect for him, plus I loved the fact that I knew exactly what went into them!

breakfast

egg in the hole

2 servings

2 sandwich bread slices

1 tablespoon unsalted butter

2 large eggs

Kosher salt

As a cook, I get bored making the same thing day after day, but I went through a long breakfast stretch in which Kenya and Chloe wanted omelets for *every* breakfast. I began going a bit nutty from the "crack eggs, whisk eggs, cook eggs" routine, so I decided to see how they'd respond to a bit of change.

Egg in the Hole was one of my favorite breakfasts growing up. It's an especially great dish to cook with kids because there's so much fun stuff they can do to help you prepare it, but getting to make the holes in the bread is probably the most fun for them. When I was little, a simple drinking glass was the perfect hole-maker. But here at weelicious, we believe things can always be even more fun, and cookie cutters aren't *just* for making cookies, you know.

While you're getting everything ready to prepare this dish, let your kids rummage through your cookie cutters to pick the shape they want their egg hole to be. I love that every kid can personalize his or her breakfast any way they want, so say hello to Egg in the Witch, Egg in the Gingerbread Man, Egg in the Star, and more!

1. Using a cookie cutter, press out the center of the pieces of bread, reserving the cutouts.

2. Heat a large sauté pan over medium heat and melt the butter.

3. Add the pieces of bread and the center cutouts to the pan.

4. Break 1 egg into each cutout, sprinkle with salt to taste, and cook for 2 to 3 minutes, until set.

5. Flip the bread gently and cook to the desired doneness, 3 to 4 minutes total for runny eggs and 7 minutes total for firm eggs.

6. Serve each Egg in the Hole with the toasted cutout for dipping in the yolk.

LESLEY: I make my kids Egg in the Hole for supper on evenings when there's not much time. They love them and think they're super-cute. Plus, a slice of whole wheat bread and an egg are healthy for them to eat, and so quick and easy to make. We use different cookie cutters to mix it up—teddy bears, hearts, Christmas cutters at holiday time. I've even made "omelets in the hole" and added cheese and veggies!

BECKY: Egg in the Hole is how I got my son to start eating eggs! While he'll only eat them scrambled, I can now get him to eat them "out of the hole."

NIKKI: My daughter was so picky about eggs until we discovered the secret of Egg in the Hole. I can cook them any way as long as they're tucked into a heart-shaped hole!

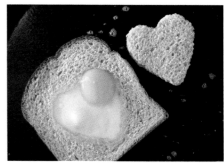

blueberry-lemon whole wheat pancakes

4 servings

1⅓ cups whole wheat flour

1 teaspoon baking powder

½ teaspoon baking soda

½ teaspoon salt

2 tablespoons vegetable or canola oil, plus more for cooking

1 large egg

1 cup milk

1 tablespoon honey

1 tablespoon fresh lemon juice

1 teaspoon lemon zest

1 cup fresh or frozen unthawed blueberries

Maple syrup, honey, butter, or Raspberr-Wee Sauce (page 117)

One of the benefits of living in Los Angeles is that there's free fruit everywhere. Here in LA, if a fruit tree is growing on or over public property, you can pick as much as you want. The kids love going for walks in our neighborhood and returning home with a bag full of the oranges and kumquats that grow wild near us. One of our friends has an enormous lemon tree at her house, and she brings dozens over to us weekly, so I'm always trying to think of fun uses for them.

Blueberry pancakes are delicious, but add some lemon and they become something truly fabulous. The lemon adds a unique zip and zing and totally brightens the flavor of pancakes. Now if I could only find a free blueberry bush . . .

1. In a large bowl, whisk together the flour, baking powder, baking soda, and salt.

2. In a medium bowl, whisk together the oil, egg, milk, honey, lemon juice, and lemon zest.

3. Whisk the dry ingredients into the wet ingredients until just combined (it's okay if there are a few lumps).

4. Heat a large pan or griddle over medium heat and grease with oil.

5. Pour about 1 heaping tablespoon of the pancake batter onto the griddle and top with 2 to 3 blueberries. Repeat to make more pancakes.

6. Cook the pancakes for 2 minutes, then flip and cook for 2 minutes more.

7. Serve with maple syrup, honey, butter, or Raspberr-Wee Sauce.

breakfast cupcakes

20 mini cupcakes (this batter can also be used to make pancakes)

1¼ cups all-purpose flour

2 teaspoons baking powder

½ teaspoon salt

¼ cup peanut, almond, cashew, or sunflower butter

1 large egg

2 tablespoons sugar

1¼ cups milk

Breakfast Cupcake "Frosting" (recipe follows)

Cupcakes for breakfast. Mothers all over America probably will want to strangle me right now. That is, until they taste these cupcakes.

This recipe was a happy accident. I had been working on some creative, out-of-the-box PB&J school lunch recipes and thought the idea of peanut butter pancake sandwiches with preserves in the middle sounded like something I would have flipped for as a kid. I tested the recipe several times to get it right, and I still had a ton of batter leftover afterward. I hate wasting food, but I was too lazy to stand around making a hundred pancakes. Just to see what would happen, I poured all the remaining batter into some mini muffin pans and popped them into the oven.

I couldn't believe the results. Why hadn't I thought of this before? They'd become the perfect breakfast "muffin," as Chloe called it, or "cupcake," as Kenya chimed in. A lightbulb went off—what kid wouldn't eat his breakfast if it was called a cupcake?! Inspired to take things one step further, I whisked together some strawberry preserves and cream cheese to make the "icing" and—voilà—the Breakfast Cupcake was born!

These cupcakes are light and fluffy like a pancake, and with the airy "frosting" it's a treat you can happily serve any time of day, and your little one will adore them. The best part is that you'll have a new morning surprise for your family—and they'll never know these cupcakes aren't loaded with sugar. Accidents happen, and boy can they be delicious!

SHANNON: The first time I made Breakfast Cupcakes, my three-year-old looked at me as if I'd lost my mind. "This is my breakfast? Not my dessert?" she asked, with eyes as big as the cupcakes. She loves telling people she had a cupcake for breakfast—and I love knowing how good it is for her little body.

1. Preheat the oven to 350°F and grease a mini muffin pan.

2. In a medium bowl, whisk together the flour, baking soda, and salt.

3. In a separate medium bowl, whisk the nut butter, egg, and sugar until combined, then whisk in the milk until incorporated.

4. Whisk the dry ingredients into the wet ingredients until just combined—do not overmix.

5. Fill the muffin cups two thirds of the way up with the batter.

6. Bake for 20 minutes, or until a toothpick comes out clean.

7. Cool and spread the top of each cupcake with frosting.

breakfast cupcake "frosting"

Combine the ingredients in a bowl and whisk until smooth.

**makes about
2 cups**

½ cup whipped or regular cream cheese, softened

¼ cup of your favorite jelly, jam, or preserves

cottage cheese pancakes

20 to 25 pancakes

3 large eggs

1 cup cottage cheese

1 teaspoon pure vanilla extract

2 tablespoons honey or agave nectar

½ cup all-purpose flour

1 teaspoon baking powder

¼ teaspoon salt

Unsalted butter or canola or vegetable oil, for the pan

Pure maple syrup or honey, for serving

Even when you're as committed to good nutrition as I am, kids are kids and not easily swayed by their parents' preferences. For instance, Kenya does not like cottage cheese. I've tried (and repeatedly failed) to make it appealing to him in countless ways. I've topped it with Raspberr-Wee Sauce (page 117), let him squeeze honey on it, mixed it with diced pineapple (one of my favorite childhood combinations), and attempted many other variations, but each time he takes a bite he refuses to eat any more. I embrace and respect the fact that every kid has his own unique palate and that Kenya may just not like cottage cheese, but I still wasn't ready to give up on it. Packed with protein, cottage cheese is such a nutritious food (and reasonably inexpensive) that I became driven to use it to create a recipe Kenya would enjoy.

These pancakes were finally born after many noble attempts, so I was excited to see what Kenya's response would be. *Six* pancakes into his breakfast, he asked, "What kind of pancakes are these, Mommy?" I felt as if I'd been caught (as you know, I'm on the record as saying we shouldn't sneak foods to our kids). I hesitantly mumbled, "Cottage cheese pancakes." He just looked at me and said, "They're really good," and he's viewed cottage cheese differently ever since. Just goes to show that when it comes to food, don't give up on something you believe your kids will ultimately love.

1. In a medium bowl, whisk together the eggs, cottage cheese, vanilla, and honey.

2. In a small bowl, whisk together the flour, baking powder, and salt.

3. Pour the dry mixture into the wet mixture and stir until just combined.

4. Heat a large sauté pan or griddle over medium heat, lightly coat it with butter or oil, and pour about 1 tablespoon of the mixture onto the griddle for each pancake.

5. Cook for 2 minutes on each side, or until the pancakes are set and golden.

6. Serve with pure maple syrup or honey.

TIP: *These pancakes can be frozen for up to 3 months. Just let them cool to room temperature and place them in a labeled zip-top bag.*

MELISSA: **Your Cottage Cheese Pancakes are a staple in our house. I make a huge batch and freeze them. The second the last pancake is eaten, another batch is made. I can never be without them. My eighteen-month-old loves them, and with the protein, it's an awesome breakfast.**

LISA: **We love, love, love the Cottage Cheese Pancakes. I make them for my twenty-one-month-old all the time. Okay, I admit it, I eat most of them.**

LORI: **We eat them all the time now, and cottage cheese isn't a scary concept around here anymore!**

JEN: **I believe we are single-handedly supporting the cottage cheese industry with how often I make these for my son. He's been eating them since he started solids (they're a perfect baby-led weaning food!) and still can't get enough of them at twenty months. The best part is that I never feel bad giving them to him, because they're so healthy.**

slow-cooker apple streusel oatmeal

4 to 6 servings

1 cup steel-cut oats

2 ½ cups milk

1 teaspoon ground cinnamon

2 cups diced Granny Smith apples

½ cup chopped walnuts

½ cup raisins

Fruit and Seed Granola (page 85, or your favorite store-bought brand)

Have you ever made oatmeal in a slow cooker? If the answer is no, now is the time to get on it! This recipe totally changed my mornings and turned me from stressed out short-order cook to super-popular mommy with the fam. A slow cooker is one of the best kitchen investments you can make, especially if you have kids. It virtually does all the work for you. Just toss all the ingredients in the slow cooker the night before, turn it on, and in the morning your house will smell just like warm apple pie. And taste twice as scrumptious.

1. Place the oats, milk, cinnamon, apples, walnuts, raisins, and 2 cups water in a slow cooker and stir to combine.

2. Turn the slow cooker to low heat and cook for 4 hours (the amount of time can vary depending on your cooker), then switch to the warm setting until you are ready to serve.

3. Top with the granola and serve.

JEN: Our family makes this regularly. How nice (not to mention convenient) to wake up to the delicious smell of oatmeal cooking in the morning.

MICHELLE: Thanks for the awesome recipe! It was a hit with my husband, who doesn't normally get excited about oatmeal, so I'm super excited about it!

red, white, and blue parfaits

I am addicted to Grape-Nuts and have been for years. There's just something about the nutty, crunchy taste that I can't get enough of. When I was pregnant with both Kenya and Chloe I ate a gigantic bowl every day, so it's no wonder they are totally hooked on them as well.

I try to make this dish first thing in the morning, so that by the time the kids are ready for breakfast the Grape-Nuts have gotten a chance to soften up from the yogurt. The two of them have so much fun taking their spoons, pushing them deep in the glass, and pulling up delectable, multicolored bites of pure yumminess.

For each serving, layer in a glass:

1 tablespoon Grape-Nuts
1 tablespoon yogurt
2 tablespoons blueberries
1 tablespoon Grape-Nuts
1 tablespoon yogurt
2 tablespoons raspberries

TIP: Instead of Grape-Nuts you can substitute your favorite cereal, muesli, or Fruit and Seed Granola (page 85).

2 servings

¼ cup Grape-Nuts cereal

¼ cup plain yogurt

¼ cup fresh raspberries, chopped if desired

¼ cup fresh blueberries, chopped if desired

breakfast quesadilla

1 large quesadilla, serves 2

2 large eggs

1 teaspoon vegetable or canola oil

¼ cup shredded Mexican-blend cheese (or you can use Cheddar, Monterey Jack, or mozzarella)

2 large white, whole wheat, or spelt tortillas (if you use small tortillas, use 1 egg per quesadilla and ¼ cup cheese)

Salsa, pico de gallo, ketchup, and/or cilantro, for serving (optional)

You would think someone who cooks as much as I do would have a fridge full of food 24/7. Although I do try to keep my larder well stocked, there are many weeks when I'm running around nonstop and don't have time to get to the grocery to pick up our everyday essentials. Still, there are three things that I *always* have on hand: eggs, tortillas, and cheese. They're all relatively inexpensive, last for weeks if properly refrigerated, and combine to make the perfect breakfast meal that will send your kids off to school with tons of energy for their day.

I had originally tried making this Breakfast Quesadilla with scrambled eggs, but when it came time to eat it, huge chunks of eggs kept falling out of the tortillas and onto the floor. No one dislikes cleaning up more than I do, so I went back to the drawing board and experimented—this time cooking the eggs like a thin omelet, topping each side with melted cheese, and then sandwiching it all between two tortillas.

My kids love this recipe so much, it's gone into heavy morning breakfast rotation at my house. That's good news for me, especially since I just checked and my fridge is practically bare again!

1. In a medium bowl, whisk the eggs for 30 seconds, or until fluffy.

2. Heat the oil in a 9-inch sauté pan over medium heat, swirling to coat the bottom of the pan. Make sure to use a pan that is at least slightly larger than your tortilla.

3. Pour in the eggs, tilting the pan to spread them evenly across the surface. Cook the omelet for 30 seconds, then gently use a spatula to loosen the edges away from the sides of the pan.

4. Sprinkle 2 tablespoons of the cheese on top of the omelet and place 1 tortilla on top of the egg and cheese. Place a plate upside down over the part and carefully flip the pan and plate to turn the quesadilla over.

5. Slide the omelet, tortilla side-down, back into the pan. Sprinkle the remaining 2 tablespoons cheese on top of the egg and top with the second tortilla.

6. Cook the quesadilla for 1 minute, pressing down lightly with a spatula to help melt the cheese. Flip the quesadilla to cook the other side for 30 seconds, or until the cheese melts and the tortilla is golden.

7. Cut into wedges and serve with any of the condiments.

🖥 baby frittatas

12 baby frittatas

3 large eggs

2 tablespoons milk

2 tablespoons grated Parmesan cheese

¼ cup diced asparagus

3 oil-packed sun-dried tomatoes, diced

Baked in mini muffin cups, these baby frittatas are so cute I want to squeeze them like I squeeze my kids' tushies!

They're not only petite and cute; they're also delicious. Each baby frittata is loaded with protein from the eggs and vitamins from the two vegetables, making them really nutritious. With the addition of Parmesan for savory flavor and sun-dried tomatoes for a little tang, these baby frittatas will be a hit with everyone in the family, not just your kids.

Whether you're making them for breakfast or serving them at a party as hors d'oeuvres, everyone, young and old, will adore them.

1. Preheat the oven to 375°F and spray or grease 12 mini muffin cups with oil or butter.

ALIZA: **I'm always trying to keep breakfast interesting for my year-old son. I'm a teacher and leave too early to have breakfast with him, and I'm always looking to freeze things so that he has variety, since my husband doesn't cook breakfast. The Baby Frittatas are a big hit with my son, and his daddy loves them too! They're very versatile because you can add anything—and they freeze well, too!**

INES: **The first time my son ate eggs and liked them was when he was fourteen months old and I made him Baby Frittatas. He ate five—he tried to stuff them into his mouth whole! I was so excited that I'd finally found a way for him to like eggs.**

2. In a medium bowl, whisk the eggs and milk together. Stir in the remaining ingredients.

3. Place a heaping tablespoon of the egg/vegetable mixture in each muffin cup.

4. Bake for 12 to 14 minutes, until golden and set.

5. Cool before serving.

french toast sticks

One of our missions at weelicious is to offer recipes the entire family can enjoy together. A few simple alterations to almost any dish suited for Mommy and Daddy will make it totally attractive to kids as well. Take these French Toast Sticks, for example. It's not that I couldn't simply hand Chloe an entire piece of French toast and have her eat it—she's actually such an adventurous eater, she'll hoover just about anything—but tailoring a breakfast food my husband and I eat with a knife and fork to give it a fun and appealing kid-friendly shape allows everyone in our family to enjoy the same meal in their own way.

These little French toast "fingers" are not only delicious, they're also the perfect size for little hands to hold. Kenya loves dipping them into Raspberr-Wee Sauce (page 117), Chloe loves that she can eat them independently, and I love that you get *triple* the crusty edges for each piece, since you cut each piece of bread into three sticks. There's truly nothing better than a recipe that meets everyone's needs!

1. In a shallow bowl, whisk the eggs, milk, cinnamon, honey, and salt until combined.

2. Dip each bread stick in the egg mixture, coating both sides.

3. Heat the butter in a sauté pan or griddle over medium heat. Working in batches, cook the French Toast Sticks for 3 minutes on each side, or until golden and cooked through.

4. Serve with the Raspberr-Wee Sauce, honey, or maple syrup.

15 sticks

2 large eggs

½ cup milk

½ teaspoon ground cinnamon

2 teaspoons honey or agave nectar

Pinch of salt

5 slices sandwich bread, crusts trimmed off, each cut into 1-inch sticks

1 tablespoon unsalted butter

Raspberr-Wee Sauce (page 117), honey, or pure maple syrup, for serving

ERIKA: **I made French Toast Sticks for my daughter when she was entering the finger food stage. They were perfect for her to grab and eat on her own without my help. The softness of the bread also helped her eat them without struggling to chew too much— it basically melted in her mouth. She's two now and still loves French Toast Sticks!**

📺 stuffed french toast

4 servings

½ cup raspberry preserves

8 slices bread, crusts cut off

4 ounces (½ cup) cream cheese, softened

3 large eggs

⅓ cup milk

1 tablespoon pure maple syrup

Pinch of salt

Butter, for greasing the pan

Maple syrup or honey, for serving

Kenya's class at school learns to cook together on occasion, and he gets such a thrill from it. One of his favorites so far has been French toast. After weeks of him asking me to make it for breakfast, I tried out this new version on him, and he went gaga for it. Stuffed with cream cheese and raspberry preserves, it's a little bit different from the French toast Kenya's used to, but the smile on his face after he took his first bite convinced me that the next time they make French toast at school, Kenya's going to be teaching all his friends how to put a spin on it!

1. Spread 2 tablespoons of the preserves in the center of 4 slices of the bread.

2. Spread 2 tablespoons of the cream cheese on the outer edges of 4 slices of bread.

3. Make 4 sandwiches, each with both cream cheese and preserves.

4. In a shallow bowl, whisk the eggs, milk, maple syrup, and salt to combine.

5. In a large sauté pan over medium heat, melt the butter.

6. Dip each side of the sandwiches in the egg-milk mixture to thoroughly coat.

7. Cook the stuffed French toast over medium heat for 3 to 4 minutes on each side, until golden.

8. Serve with maple syrup or honey.

oatmeal on-the-go bars

18 bars

2 cups old-fashioned rolled oats (not steel-cut and not quick-cooking)

1 cup whole wheat flour

1½ teaspoons ground cinnamon

Pinch of salt

1 teaspoon baking powder

1½ cups milk

½ cup applesauce

1 large egg

3 tablespoons honey or agave nectar

1 teaspoon pure vanilla extract

¾ cup dried fruit, such as cranberries, raisins, blueberries, and/or cherries

½ cup nuts or seeds, such as walnuts, sunflower seeds, and/or pepitas

I eat oatmeal *every* day. I'm actually eating a bowl of it as I write this—no joke. Oatmeal is one of my favorite foods, not only because it's heart healthy and nutritious but also because it's filling and beyond easy to make—perfect for moms that are constantly on the go. But I'm not the only one in our house who loves oatmeal. Kenya and Chloe ask for oatmeal for breakfast as often as they ask for pancakes, omelets, and waffles.

I wanted to come up with a recipe using oatmeal that would be perfect for those days you're racing out the door and don't have time to cook. (I think that's most mornings for many of us.) I liked the idea of breakfast bars because almost every mom I know seems to have a stash of LARA BARS, or Clif or Odwalla bars in her tote bag. These Oatmeal On-the-Go Bars don't try to duplicate those bars—they're essentially just oatmeal in bar form—but they're equally delicious. Just prepare a batch, keep them in the fridge, and grab a few on your way out and you're set.

For all of you "on-the-go" moms, this bar's for you.

1. Preheat the oven to 375°F and grease a 7 x 11-inch baking dish.

2. In a medium bowl, combine the oats, flour, cinnamon, salt, and baking powder.

3. In a large bowl, whisk together the milk, applesauce, egg, honey, and vanilla.

4. Pour the dry ingredients into the wet mixture, stir until combined, and stir in the dried fruits and nuts.

5. Pour the oatmeal mixture into the baking dish and bake for 30 minutes, or until thick and golden.

6. Cool and cut into squares. The bars will last up to 5 days in the refrigerator.

TO FREEZE: *Cool, cut into squares, and place in a zip-top bag to freeze for up to 3 months. To serve, allow to defrost in the fridge for 24 hours.*

LAURA: When it was my first turn to bring in a snack for my daughter's kindergarten class, I decided I wanted to make something nutritious and filling, with quality ingredients, to get them through the rest of the day. But I wanted them to actually like and *eat* it, too. These bars were a huge hit—all week long parents were leaving notes in my daughter's folder asking me for the recipe.

MEGAN: I make your Oatmeal On-the-Go Bars all the time. I brought them to a new mom friend shortly after she gave birth, and as a nursing mom myself, I love them too!

LAURA: My four-year-old daughter, who'll usually eat only dry cereal for breakfast, will eat three or four of these bars, so I love to keep them around— she'll get more substance for breakfast. They also make a great snack for the older kids to take to school.

breakfast 77

breakfast polenta

6 to 8 servings

Olive or canola oil spray

1 teaspoon salt

One 13-ounce box instant polenta

¼ cup packed brown sugar

1 teaspoon ground cinnamon

½ teaspoon ground nutmeg

4 tablespoons unsalted butter

Pure maple syrup, honey, or Raspberr-Wee Sauce (page 117), for serving

Simple and inexpensive, you can prepare this dish ahead of time and keep it in the fridge. Just give it a quick sauté and serve with your favorite topping. Out of the ordinary, but I'm betting your family will love it!

1. Line a baking sheet with foil and coat it with olive or canola oil spray.

2. In a medium saucepan, add the salt to 7 cups of water and bring it to a boil over high heat.

3. Add the polenta in a slow stream, whisking continuously to avoid lumps.

4. Turn the heat to low and continue to stir with a wooden spoon until the polenta thickens, 5 to 8 minutes. You may add more hot water as needed to keep the polenta at a smooth consistency.

5. Turn off the heat and add the brown sugar, cinnamon, nutmeg, and 3 tablespoons of the butter. Stir to combine.

6. Pour the polenta onto the baking sheet and spread it out with the back of a spoon to cover the sheet evenly (it will be about 1 inch thick).

7. Refrigerate the polenta for at least 30 minutes or up to 24 hours.

8. Remove from the refrigerator and use cookie cutters to stamp out fun shapes. And you the parent get to eat all the polenta scraps. Yum!

9. Heat the remaining 1 tablespoon butter in a large sauté pan over medium heat. Working in batches, cook the polenta shapes for 3 to 5 minutes on each side, until golden. Serve.

TO FREEZE: *After step 8, the polenta shapes can be frozen for up to 3 months in labeled zip-top bags. Defrost at room temperature for 30 minutes and cook according to step 9.*

NOTE: *Polenta will keep, covered, in the refrigerator for 1 week. To reheat, place in a sauté pan and cook over low heat for 2 minutes on each side or in a toaster oven for 2 minutes.*

pumpkin waffles

In our house, I'm all about serving these waffles for breakfast, but I decided to take them one step further. I usually like to make a big batch, enjoy half right then, freeze a bunch for future breakfasts, and then make sandwiches with what's left. Yes, sandwiches. How excited will your kids be when they open their lunch box to see cream cheese (and maybe some sliced fruit) between two fluffy Pumpkin Waffles? I guarantee you'll win Mom (or Dad) of the Year for that one!

1. Preheat a waffle iron.

2. Sift the flour, baking powder, baking soda, salt, cinnamon, and ginger into a large bowl.

3. In a separate large bowl, whisk the eggs, brown sugar, milk, buttermilk, pumpkin puree, and butter.

4. Whisk the dry ingredients into the liquid mixture and whisk until smooth.

5. Butter the hot waffle iron. Pour about ½ cup of the pumpkin batter into the waffle iron and cook according to the manufacturer's directions.

6. Serve with maple syrup.

TO FREEZE: *Cool to room temperature, place in a zip-top bag, label, and freeze for up to 3 months. To serve, place in a preheated 300°F oven or a toaster oven and heat for 10 minutes, or until heated through.*

TIP: *Make a waffle sandwich with a filling of cream cheese, jam, nut butter, or whatever you like!*

twelve 4-inch waffles

2 ½ cups all-purpose flour

2 ½ teaspoons baking powder

1 teaspoon baking soda

½ teaspoon salt

2 teaspoons ground cinnamon

1 teaspoon ground ginger

4 large eggs

⅓ cup packed light or dark brown sugar

1 cup milk

1 cup buttermilk (or use a scant cup of milk combined with 1 tablespoon white vinegar or lemon juice; allow to sit for 5 minutes before adding)

1 cup pumpkin puree (not pie filling)

6 tablespoons (¾ stick) unsalted butter, melted and cooled, plus a bit for the waffle iron

Pure maple syrup, for serving

breakfast pizza pockets

8 servings

4 large eggs

½ teaspoon kosher salt

1 teaspoon vegetable or canola oil

1 cup grated mozzarella cheese

¼ cup, finely chopped cooked bacon or ham

1 package whole wheat or white pizza dough, brought to room temperature

½ cup marinara sauce

OPTIONAL FILLINGS

Sausage, veggie dogs, mushrooms, bell pepper, onion, or any veggies you have on hand

PROBLEM: On those mornings when everyone "decides" to sleep in, I rise rested and exhilarated . . . until I realize that we all have to be out the door in forty-five minutes and I still haven't made breakfast. As much as I would like to be Carol Brady in the kitchen every morning, whipping up a home-made meal for the family, I cherish every bit of sleep my kids let me have, so sadly it doesn't happen that often.

SOLUTION: Quickly turn the oven on, get the crew dressed, take Breakfast Pizza Pockets from the freezer, pop them in the oven, make the beds, pack lunches, feed everyone their Breakfast Pizza Pockets, and get them out the door. Thank goodness I can rely on my freezer to help provide my family with a fresh breakfast.

Now that I think of it, maybe I shouldn't feel so bad. Mrs. Brady had Alice. But she didn't have these delicious pizza pockets.

1. Preheat the oven to 450°F and line a baking sheet with parchment paper or a Silpat.

2. In a medium bowl, whisk the eggs, salt, and 1 tablespoon of water.

3. Heat the oil in a skillet over medium heat and cook the eggs until lightly scrambled, stirring often with a spoon or spatula. Set aside to cool.

4. In another bowl, combine the cooled eggs, cheese, and bacon or ham bits. Set aside.

5. Divide the dough into 8 equal pieces and roll out each piece into 4 x 8-inch rectangles.

6. Divide the egg mixture into 8 portions—one for each pizza pocket.

7. Spread about 1 tablespoon of sauce evenly over 1 dough rectangle. Place a portion of the egg mixture on one side of the dough.

8. Bring opposite sides of the dough together and press to form a square.

9. Place the pockets on the baking sheet and bake for 18 minutes, or until golden.

10. Cool slightly and serve.

TO FREEZE: *After step 8, place the pockets on a baking sheet and freeze for 1 hour. Remove and place the pockets in a zip-top bag, label, and freeze for up to 3 months. When ready to eat, follow steps 9 and 10, adding an extra 3 minutes to the baking time.*

bacon and cheese waffles

We don't eat a lot of bacon in our house, but whenever the grandparents are in town, they order it when we go out to brunch. Kenya and Chloe go nuts for it.

Since I believe in moderation in all things, and I didn't want to totally withhold a food I loved to eat from my Southern childhood, I created a recipe that has several of their favorite foods all in one. My husband says it's the perfect solution when you're not sure whether you want a savory or sweet breakfast, as it delivers on both!

1. Preheat a waffle iron.

2. In a medium bowl, combine the flour, baking powder, baking soda, and salt and whisk to combine.

3. Add the cheese and bacon and mix to coat with the flour mixture (this will help to avoid clumping).

4. In a large bowl, whisk the eggs, milk, and oil.

5. Add the dry ingredients to the wet mixture and whisk just until combined, taking care not to overmix (which will make for tough waffles).

6. Grease the hot waffle iron. Pour about ½ cup of the batter into the waffle iron and cook 3 to 5 minutes, or until the waffles are golden and the cheese is melted. Repeat with the rest of the batter.

7. Serve with maple syrup or honey.

TO FREEZE: *After the waffles have cooled, place in a zip-top bag, label, and freeze for up to 3 months. When you're ready to eat them, defrost or pop into a toaster oven or 300°F oven for 10 minutes.*

4 to 6 servings

2 cups all-purpose flour

2 teaspoons baking powder

1 teaspoon baking soda

½ teaspoon salt

1 cup grated Cheddar cheese

½ cup finely chopped cooked bacon

2 large eggs

1½ cups milk

3 tablespoons vegetable or canola oil, plus a bit for the waffle iron

Maple syrup or honey, for serving

ACCOMPANIMENTS

Ham and scrambled eggs

banana-corn fritters

**20 fritters,
4 to 6 servings**

¾ cup cornmeal

½ cup all-purpose flour

1 teaspoon baking
powder

½ teaspoon salt

1 teaspoon ground
cinnamon

3 medium ripe bananas

2 tablespoons milk

1 large egg

Kernels from 1 ear of
corn, or ½ cup frozen
corn, defrosted

Canola or vegetable oil,
as needed

Honey, for serving

If there's one fruit I keep in the house year-round, it's bananas. Since they start to get spots and turn brown after only a few days (and I abhor wasting food), I'm constantly trying to come up with new recipes using one of our favorite potassium-filled fruits.

As much as we may try, we can't always have dinner together as a family, so breakfast is the one time of day we all share a meal. Every morning, before the demands of work and school begin, we try to cook something together. This fritter recipe is a great one for getting your kids involved, because they can peel and mash the bananas while you're measuring the remaining ingredients. And they cook fast—within minutes you'll be enjoying sweet, golden cakes. We love to top them with or dip them in sweet gooey honey.

1. In a medium bowl, combine the cornmeal, flour, baking powder, salt, and cinnamon and whisk to combine.

2. In a large bowl, mash the bananas and add the milk and egg. Whisk to combine.

3. Add the cornmeal mixture and the corn to the banana mixture and whisk until smooth.

4. Place about 1 tablespoon of oil in a large sauté pan over medium heat.

5. Working in batches, for each fritter, drop 2 tablespoons (⅛ cup) of the batter into the pan. Cook the fritters for 3 minutes on each side, or until golden. Add more oil to the pan as needed.

6. Drizzle with honey and serve.

TO FREEZE: *Cool the fritters, then place them in zip-top bags, label, and freeze for up to 3 months. When you're ready to eat them, place them in a toaster oven or 300°F oven for 10 minutes, or until heated through.*

fruit and seed granola

I like to put granola in Kenya's and Chloe's school lunches on top of yogurt, over applesauce, in a bowl with some milk, or just on its own, but since there are so many nut-free schools these days, I decided to make this tasty nut-free version. Seeds are packed with protein, so they're a great choice for kids needing an extra boost during the day.

1. Preheat the oven to 275°F and grease a large rimmed baking sheet.

2. Place the oil, honey, oats, wheat germ, pumpkin seeds, sunflower seeds, and sesame seeds in a large bowl. Stir until evenly coated.

3. Spread the mixture evenly on the baking sheet and bake for 45 minutes.

4. Remove the granola from the oven and stir. Spread the mixture evenly again and bake for 45 minutes more, or until golden.

5. Stir the granola mixture, add the coconut flakes and dried fruit, spread the mixture on the cookie sheet once more, and let it cool thoroughly on the sheet. Do not stir—you'll get nice chunks that are like a delicious, seed-filled candy bar.

6. Break apart the granola and serve.

TO STORE: *Place the granola in an airtight container or zip-top bag.*

12 servings

½ cup canola or vegetable oil

½ cup honey

2½ cups old-fashioned oats (not instant and not steel-cut)

¼ cup wheat germ

1 cup raw pumpkin seeds

1 cup raw sunflower seeds

¼ cup raw sesame seeds

1½ cups unsweetened coconut flakes

1 cup chopped dried apricots

1 cup chopped dried cherries

apple-vanilla pancakes

about 30 mini pancakes, 6 servings

1 cup finely diced apple (preferably Gala or Pink Lady)

½ teaspoon ground cinnamon

1 packed tablespoon brown sugar

1⅓ cups all-purpose flour

2 ½ teaspoons baking powder

½ teaspoon salt

2 tablespoons vegetable oil

1¼ cups buttermilk (or use a scant 1¼ cups milk combined with 1 tablespoon white vinegar or lemon juice; allow to sit for 5 minutes before adding)

2 large eggs

½ vanilla bean or 1 teaspoon pure vanilla extract

Butter or vegetable oil, for the pan

Maple syrup or honey, for serving

When I ask the kids what they want for breakfast, often the answer is pancakes. Whether you're making these pancakes for a one-year-old or a forty-year-old, they're a real treat. Filled with cubes of apples and a fresh vanilla flavor, these are truly exceptional.

When I'm really pressed for time to make school lunch, I spread two mini pancakes left over from breakfast with cream cheese and apple butter for a unique sandwich that will be the envy of the other kids at school.

1. In a medium bowl, combine the apple, cinnamon, and brown sugar.

2. In a large bowl, combine the flour, baking powder, and salt.

3. In a separate medium bowl, whisk together the oil, buttermilk, and eggs.

4. Slice the vanilla bean in half lengthwise, scrape the vanilla seeds out with the side of your knife, add them to the buttermilk mixture, and whisk to combine (or add the vanilla extract and whisk to combine).

5. Slowly add the flour mixture to the wet mixture and stir until just combined, to avoid making tough pancakes.

6. Lightly fold the apple mixture into the batter.

7. Heat a large pan or griddle over medium heat and grease with butter.

8. Working in batches, for each pancake, pour about 2 tablespoons (⅛ cup) of the batter onto the pan or griddle.

9. Cook for 2 to 3 minutes on each side, until golden.

10. Serve with maple syrup or honey.

TO FREEZE: *Place the pancakes in zip-top freezer bags, label, and freeze for up to 3 months.*

soup

chicken tortilla soup

4 to 6 servings

1 tablespoon olive oil

1 small onion, diced (about 1 cup)

1 teaspoon kosher salt

1 red bell pepper, diced

1 small garlic clove, minced

1 teaspoon ground cumin

One 32-ounce box low-sodium chicken broth

1 bay leaf

1½ cups frozen corn kernels

One 15-ounce can diced tomatoes

1 pound boneless, skinless chicken breasts

Juice of 1 lime

Crushed tortilla chips, for serving

OPTIONAL ACCOMPANIMENTS

Shredded Monterey Jack or Mexican cheese blend, avocado, sour cream, cilantro, diced green onions

For someone who loves to cook as much as I do, there are days, plenty of them in fact, when I just want a delicious dinner to appear magically before my eyes (or at least require as little work as possible). This soup is the answer to my prayers. With just a tiny bit of effort, I'm able to get this flavorful soup on the table for my family.

For starters, who doesn't like tortilla chips? The first time I put Kenya's and Chloe's bowls in front of them with some tortilla chips on the side, their eyes lit up. They loved that I let them use their hands to break up the crunchy chips and ribbons of grated cheese to sprinkle on top of the soup so they could then stir them in, making dinner not only an interactive experience, but a delectable one at that!

1. In a large saucepan or Dutch oven, heat the oil over medium heat. Add the onion and sauté for 3 to 4 minutes, or until softened.

2. Add the salt, bell pepper, garlic, and cumin and sauté for 2 minutes.

3. Add the broth, bay leaf, corn, tomatoes, and chicken. Bring to a boil, then lower the heat to low and simmer for 10 to 15 minutes, until the chicken breasts are cooked through.

4. Remove the chicken from the pot, set aside to cool for a minute or two, and use two forks to shred the meat. Place the shredded chicken back into the pot, add the lime juice, and simmer for 2 to 3 minutes to heat the chicken through. Remove the bay leaf.

5. Pour the soup into bowls and top with crushed tortilla chips. Serve with the desired toppings on the side.

AMY: I made this soup a couple of weeks ago and it was amazing! It was the first soup that everyone in my house ate.

ANDREA: Chicken Tortilla Soup is awesome! It's a great meal to whip up on our busiest evenings. I like to make it in our rice cooker a couple of hours before dinner and keep it warm until we're ready to eat. Thanks for this delicious, time-efficient soup that's become our family's favorite.

MARY: The kids love it—crushing tortilla chips and adding cheese is their favorite. A huge hit with the extended family as well!

carrot-ginger soup

When my best friend and I were living together, long before I was married, this soup was in my weekly recipe rotation. Like many kids who shun their veggies, my friend, who was a longtime picky eater, was hard to cook for, but she absolutely loved this naturally sweet soup.

Preparation takes minimal effort, and once Kenya saw me take out my hand blender, I don't think he cared how the soup tasted as long as he got to help me make it. Once the ingredients were cooked and nice and tender, Kenya pureed everything up, making the soup super-creamy (without using any dairy, mind you). I think he pureed it for what felt like twenty minutes until he finally deemed it "just right, Mommy."

1. In a medium saucepan or Dutch oven over medium heat, heat the oil. Add the onion and sauté for 4 to 5 minutes, until translucent.

2. Add the carrots, ginger, salt, and broth and bring the mixture to a boil. Reduce the heat to low and simmer for 15 to 20 minutes, until the carrots are fork-tender.

3. Puree the soup in a blender or with a hand blender until creamy and smooth.

4. Serve, topped with a dollop of yogurt, sour cream, or crème fraîche if desired.

TIP: *If you're pureeing the soup in a blender, keep the top slightly ajar and start the motor on the lowest possible setting so the soup doesn't explode out the top.*

4 servings

1 tablespoon olive oil

1 small yellow onion, diced (about 1 cup)

One 16-ounce bag baby carrots

2 tablespoons chopped fresh ginger

1 teaspoon kosher salt

One 32-ounce box low-sodium vegetable or chicken broth

OPTIONAL
ACCOMPANIMENTS

Plain yogurt, sour cream, or crème fraîche

PRISCILLA: Your Carrot-Ginger Soup has made a carrot lover out of a carrot hater. Me!

chicken wonton soup

4 servings

FILLING

½ pound ground chicken

¼ cup grated carrot

1 small garlic clove, minced

1 scallion, chopped

½ teaspoon grated fresh ginger

1 tablespoon low-sodium soy sauce

1 teaspoon toasted sesame oil

1 egg white

One 12-ounce package wonton wrappers (find them in the refrigerated section at your grocery)

BROTH

1 tablespoon toasted sesame oil

2 teaspoons minced fresh ginger

2 small garlic cloves, minced

Two 32-ounce boxes low-sodium chicken broth

1 tablespoon low-sodium soy sauce

2 cups chopped bok choy

2 scallions, chopped

1 tablespoon rice wine vinegar

I never would have imagined how much kids could love soup until I had my little ones and witnessed it with my own eyes. One of my friends told me that she makes homemade wonton soup for her kids almost every week, and it always vanishes. When I saw Kenya and Chloe joyfully slurping their broth and biting into the tender wontons, I knew exactly what she meant.

1. To make the wontons, place all the ingredients except the wonton wrappers in a bowl and mix thoroughly.

2. Place a large piece of parchment paper on a work surface and lay out 20 wonton wrappers.

3. Place 1 teaspoon of the chicken filling in the center of each wonton square.

4. Brush two edges of the wonton wrapper with water. Fold over to shape into a triangle, pinching the sides to seal, and set aside.

5. To make the broth, heat the sesame oil in a large saucepan or Dutch oven over medium heat. Add the ginger and garlic and sauté for 30 seconds.

6. Add the broth and soy sauce and bring to a boil over medium-high heat. Add the wontons, bok choy, scallions, and vinegar, lower the heat to medium, and simmer for 5 minutes, or until the wontons are tender.

7. Spoon out 5 wontons per serving.

TO FREEZE: *Place the uncooked wontons on a baking sheet and freeze for 1 hour. Place in labeled zip-top bags for up to 2 months. When ready to cook, follow step 5.*

QUICK TIP: *To peel ginger easily, use the edge of a teaspoon to peel off the skin before chopping.*

four-bean slow-cooker chili

8 to 10 servings

2 tablespoons
vegetable or canola oil

1 large yellow onion,
chopped (about 2 cups)

2 small garlic cloves,
minced

1 pound lean ground
beef

One 15-ounce can
white beans, rinsed
and drained

One 15-ounce can
kidney beans, rinsed
and drained

One 15-ounce can
pinto beans, rinsed and
drained

One 15-ounce can
black beans, rinsed and
drained

One 28-ounce can
diced tomatoes with
juice

Two 15-ounce cans
tomato juice

2 tablespoons chili
powder

1 tablespoon ground
cumin

2 bay leaves

2 teaspoons kosher salt

The Super Bowl wears me out. We often invite a huge crowd over to our house, and I don't want to be in the kitchen catering to everyone's needs when there are so many awesome commercials to watch—oh, yeah, and there's the football game, too!

The next time you have a Super Bowl party—or any big gathering—you must make this chili. The adults will love it, and the kids will have a blast adorning their chili bowls with tons of fixings. Kenya usually covers his with a cloud of sour cream or so much shredded cheese that you can't tell there's chili under the surface, but he inhales it all nonetheless.

Make the chili the night before or the morning of the party, and all you'll need to do when everyone shows up is hang out and enjoy the fun!

1. In a large sauté pan over medium heat, heat 1 tablespoon of the oil. Add the onion and sauté for 3 minutes, or until softened. Add the garlic and sauté 1 minute. Place the onion and garlic in a slow cooker.

2. Add the remaining 1 tablespoon oil to the sauté pan, turn the heat to medium, add the ground beef, and sauté for about 5 minutes, breaking the beef apart with a wooden spoon until it's cooked through and most of the juices have evaporated.

3. Add the cooked beef and the remaining ingredients to the slow cooker and stir to combine.

4. Cover and cook the chili on low for 8 hours.

5. Serve with the desired accompaniments.

ASHLEY: My boys love beans, so this is an easy dinner that everyone loves. I love knowing they're getting an iron-rich meal that keeps their bellies full all night with no 5 a.m. "I'm hungry" wake-up calls!

VALERIE: I make the Four-Bean Slow-Cooker Chili all the time. We're not even big chili eaters, but one day I was looking for something easy to throw in the slow cooker and I happened to have all the ingredients on hand. It seriously blew my family away! Even my two-year-old (who pretty much lives off of blueberries and waffles) was in love.

OPTIONAL ACCOMPANIMENTS

Sour cream, yogurt, grated Cheddar cheese, scallions, crushed tortilla chips, hot sauce (if you want to take it up a notch)

Variations

4 servings

FOUR-BEAN CHILI MAC AND CHEESE: In a large pot over medium heat, combine 1 cup whole milk, 2 cups grated Cheddar cheese, 2 cups chili, and ½ teaspoon salt and heat through for 3 minutes, or until the cheese melts. Stir in 2 cups cooked elbow macaroni and cook an additional 3 minutes, or until the mixture comes together and the pasta is heated through.

FOUR-BEAN CHILI SPAGHETTI: Cook ½ package of spaghetti and divide it among 4 bowls. Top each bowl with ½ cup warm chili and a handful of grated Cheddar cheese.

FOUR-BEAN CHILI FRIES: Divide Oven-Baked "Fries" (page 218) among 4 bowls and top each with ½ cup chili, plus grated Cheddar cheese, sour cream, and chopped chives, as desired.

FOUR-BEAN CHILI BAKED POTATOES: Using a fork, poke a few holes in 4 russet potatoes and bake them for 1 hour at 425°F. Cut open each potato and top it with ½ cup chili, plus grated Cheddar cheese, sour cream, and chopped chives, as desired.

italian wedding soup

4 to 6 servings

1 pound ground chicken

1 large egg

¼ cup bread crumbs

2 tablespoons grated Parmesan cheese, plus more for serving (optional)

1 teaspoon dried Italian herbs (any or all of these: dried basil, rosemary, marjoram, thyme, oregano)

1 tablespoon chopped fresh flat-leaf parsley

1 small garlic clove, minced, or ¼ teaspoon garlic powder

2 teaspoons kosher salt

1 tablespoon olive oil

1 small onion, diced

Two 32-ounce boxes low-sodium chicken broth

1 cup orzo pasta

2 cups chopped kale, spinach, and/or Swiss chard

Kids really do say the darndest things—it's a cliché for good reason. The first time I tested out this Italian Wedding Soup was for some friends who came over for a visit. As I was serving everyone, they asked if my kids really did eat anything I made for them. As Kenya and Chloe ran in and out of the kitchen, I proceeded to explain how blessed I was to have these two great eaters, but I could tell that my guests, who had young kids of their own, were dubious. Right then, as if on cue, Kenya and Chloe came in and said that they were hungry and so I ladled out two small servings of the soup. Although it's true that my kids will eat just about anything I make them, at this moment they decided for whatever reason to declare very outspokenly that they were definitely not into my new creation. My guests were tickled. I was horrified.

Later, as I was walking our guests to the door to say good-bye (and still recovering from my embarrassment), Kenya yelled out, "Mommy, you can't ever make anything but this soup." Everyone turned to look at me as if I had prodded Kenya to say this, but if you've ever tried to coach a four-year-old to give a convincing performance, you know it's not going to happen. Lo and behold, there sitting on the kitchen counter were two little empty bowls of soup.

Sometimes giving kids time to learn to love something on their own—without prodding them—can be the best recipe for success in the kitchen. Next to the recipe for this soup, of course.

1. Place the chicken, egg, bread crumbs, cheese, Italian herbs, parsley, garlic, and 1 teaspoon of the salt in a food processor and pulse to combine.

2. Form little meatballs from 1 teaspoon each of the ground chicken mixture. Set aside.

3. In a large saucepan or Dutch oven, heat the oil over medium heat. Add the onion and sauté for 4 minutes, or until softened.

4. Add the broth and bring it to a boil. Lower the heat to a simmer, add the meatballs, pasta, and remaining 1 teaspoon salt, and cook for 8 minutes, or until the meatballs are cooked through.

5. Add the greens and cook for 2 minutes, or until softened.

6. Serve with cheese sprinkled on top if desired.

chicken noodle soup

4 servings

1 tablespoon olive oil

2 carrots, peeled and chopped (about ¾ cup)

1 celery stalk, chopped (about ⅓ cup)

1 leek, white and light green parts only, halved, washed carefully, and thinly sliced (about ¾ cup)

One 32-ounce box low-sodium chicken broth

1 large boneless, skinless chicken breast

2 teaspoons Vegit or other salt-free herb seasoning

¾ cup thin egg noodles

Good for the heart, good for the soul . . . good for when everyone in our household has been sick for six days straight!

When he was two and a half, poor Kenya got a bronchial infection at a local kid play space (aka germ factory) I take him to, and within days everyone in our house was down for the count. Since there's little you can do medicinally for kids younger than age three, out came my homemade Ginger-Lemon-Honey Tea (page 265) and my personal get-better favorite, this Chicken Noodle Soup.

Almost nothing seems to taste good when you're sick, but there's something about chicken noodle soup that always makes me feel better. I've always loved this recipe because it's fast, fresh, and easy, but I've become a true pro at making it for my little "patients" during cold and flu season. It's chock-full of carrots, celery, and leeks, and it stores perfectly in the freezer, so that you're always ready. Although I love this soup, I hope we don't need it anytime soon!

1. Heat the oil in a large saucepan or Dutch oven over medium heat. Add the carrots, celery, and leek and sauté for 4 minutes, or until softened.

2. Add the broth, chicken, and Vegit and bring to a boil. Turn the heat to medium-low and simmer the soup for 12 minutes, or until the chicken is cooked through.

3. Remove the chicken breast and cool. Shred or chop into bite-size pieces.

4. Add the noodles to the broth and cook for 6 minutes, or until tender.

5. Return the chicken to the soup to warm it up. Serve.

JENNA: I made this for my thirteen-month-old daughter, who had her first little cold. It turned out great—I added a couple of minced garlic cloves. I had no idea if she was going to eat it (she'd never had soup before), but she kept signing "more" as soon as her bowl was empty—it was so cute! And I enjoyed a couple of bowls, too!

slow-cooker lentil veggie stew

When it's cold, rainy, and—hopefully—really quiet in my house, it's time for me to make warm soup to fill everyone's bellies, and that means it's time to break out my slow cooker and make lentil veggie stew. All I do is toss in some lentils, a few herbs, and a mix of vegetables from the farmers' market and serve it up with a dollop of herbed goat cheese on top—which the kids love swirling into their soup.

This recipe makes enough so that I can freeze half for those cold nights when I'm too lazy or don't have any time to cook—which seems to be most nights these days!

1. Heat the oil in a sauté pan over medium heat. Add the onion and sauté for 4 minutes, or until softened. Add the garlic and sauté for 1 minute.

2. Place the onion mixture and the remaining ingredients in a slow cooker and stir.

3. Cover and cook on high heat for 4 hours (or low heat for 8 hours), until the lentils are tender.

4. Serve with the desired accompaniments.

TIP: *You can also place all the ingredients in a large pot over medium-low to low heat, cover, and cook for 90 minutes, or until tender.*

AMY: At twelve months my son was diagnosed with multiple food allergies and a feeding disorder, and we were hard-pressed to find foods that 1) he could have and 2) he would eat! Six months later he was eating much better, but his diet was still very limited. I thought I'd give this soup a try, and he *loved* it! It was the first time he was willing to eat multiple foods together in one bite. Had I not found this recipe, I don't think I would have ever given lentils a try, and we'd be missing out on one of my three-year-old's favorite foods.

8 to 10 servings

1 tablespoon olive oil

1 large onion, chopped (about 2 cups)

2 garlic cloves, chopped

2 leeks, white and light green parts only, halved, washed carefully, and chopped

2 large carrots, peeled and chopped

3 celery stalks, chopped

2 bay leaves

1 tablespoon chopped fresh thyme or 1 teaspoon dried thyme

2 teaspoons kosher salt

8 cups low-sodium vegetable or chicken broth

One 32-ounce can diced tomatoes with juice

16 ounces dried lentils

2 cups chopped kale or Swiss chard

OPTIONAL ACCOMPANIMENTS

Plain yogurt, herbed goat cheese, feta cheese, crème fraîche, or grated Parmesan cheese

dips, sauces, and salsas

red beet and white bean hummus

3 cups

1 medium red beet

1 large garlic clove, unpeeled

One 15-ounce can white beans, rinsed and drained

Juice of ½ lemon (about ½ tablespoon)

¼ cup olive oil

1 teaspoon kosher salt

OPTIONAL ACCOMPANIMENTS

Cut-up vegetables such as bell peppers, carrots, celery, cauliflower, cucumber, and sugar snap peas, or pita chips or tortilla chips

When I first made this recipe for Kenya and Chloe, they were as fascinated by the taste as they were by the color. They kept cheering "pink food!" as they ate bowl after bowl. The ingredients are almost identical to a true hummus, minus the tahini, and the addition of the beets makes it an even more nutrient-rich dish that also provides a healthy amount of protein.

The tangy flavor and smooth and creamy texture of this dish are so mouthwatering that I think you'll find it to be a hit with kids of any age in your house. Everything from vegetables to chicken gets the dipping treatment. I served it as the centerpiece snack at Chloe's second *and* third birthday parties, and all the kids and moms were transfixed by the color. Pink food—every little girl's dream!

1. Preheat the oven to 400°F.

2. Wash the beet well and place with the garlic clove on a sheet of foil. Pull up the sides of the foil and fold to make a packet, leaving room so that heat can circulate inside.

3. Bake for 45 minutes, or until the beet is tender when poked with a knife. Set aside until cool to the touch.

4. Put a plastic bag over your hand and gently remove the skin from the beet and garlic clove. (The bag will keep your hand clean.)

5. Place all the ingredients into a food processor and puree until smooth and cooled.

6. Serve. The hummus will keep in the fridge for up to 1 week.

BJ: My fifteen-month-old is starting to get picky with her vegetables. This recipe is such a beautiful color, so I thought I would try it, and she loves it! She is working on her "big girl" motor skills, and now she's a dipping champ.

chloe's olive hummus

2 cups

One 15-ounce can garbanzo beans (chickpeas), rinsed and drained

¼ cup pitted green olives

1 small garlic clove

¼ cup pitted Kalamata olives

¼ cup olive oil

2 tablespoons tahini

3 tablespoons lemon juice

1 tablespoon balsamic vinegar

¼ teaspoon salt

OPTIONAL ACCOMPANIMENTS

Cut-up vegetables such as bell peppers, carrots, celery, cauliflower, cucumber, and sugar snap peas, or pita chips or tortilla chips

There have been times I thought Chloe might explode from eating too many olives. No joke. On several occasions our babysitter has turned help-lessly to me and said, "She won't stop eating them!" as Chloe downed one after another and screamed, *"More olives!"*

The olives Chloe likes have quite a bitter flavor, a taste most kids might turn their noses up at, but my girl loves them. So in honor of Chloe, I made this olive hummus. When mixed with the protein-packed garbanzo beans and tahini and pureed into a smooth spread, there's no bitterness what-soever and you have a dip that's delish on crackers and fresh veggies, as a sandwich spread, and even straight out of the bowl with a spoon, as Chloe demonstrated so well to me. Without exploding.

1. Place all the ingredients into a food processor and puree.

2. Serve. The hummus will keep in the fridge for up to 1 week.

sun-dried tomato and basil pesto

There are some classic things that just go great together. For some, it's Sundays and football. For others, it's chocolate and peanut butter. For me, it's food and the holidays.

We go through a ton of pesto in our house. Since basil grows wild in our garden, the kids and I like to make a new batch every few weeks to eat and give to friends. There are all different kinds of pestos, and we have lots of fun experimenting with them.

This Sun-Dried Tomato and Basil Pesto is one of my favorite gifts to make and eat, especially during the holidays. The rich red, white, and green colors couldn't make it more perfect for Christmas. Here's what I suggest:

1. Multiply the recipe and make a big batch (it's ridiculously easy to do).

2. Fill mason jars (you can get them at craft stores or most groceries) with the pesto and add your own labels with the recipe written on them so your friends can remake it if they like it (and I promise they will!).

3. Place the jars in a festive bag or basket with a box of nice pasta.

For six or seven dollars you've got a holiday gift that everyone in the family will enjoy. And it will seem like you spent much more!

1. Place all the ingredients in a food processor and blend until smooth. If the pesto is too thick, add more olive oil.

2. Serve over chicken, fish, pasta, rice, or quinoa, or mixed into Italian Corn Kernels (page 212).

TO FREEZE: *Pour the pesto into an ice-cube tray and freeze, then pop the cubes into zip-top bags. Defrost individual cubes in the fridge for 24 hours, or add a cube to hot pasta and toss until it melts.*

1½ cups

One 8.5-ounce jar sun-dried tomatoes, olive oil included

1 cup packed basil leaves

1 small garlic clove

½ cup grated Parmesan cheese

½ teaspoon salt

Olive oil, as needed

broccoli pesto

1¼ cups

1 cup broccoli florets

¼ cup toasted almond slices

¼ cup grated Parmesan cheese

1 small garlic clove

½ cup olive oil

¼ teaspoon salt

1 tablespoon lemon juice

If there's one essential mealtime item to keep on hand at all times, it has to be pesto. Even the most boring foods become truly delicious when mixed with a freshly made pesto, and with the broccoli, almonds, Parmesan, and olive oil in this recipe, you pack in a lot of added nutrition to boot. Whether I use this Broccoli Pesto on fish or chicken, spread it on a sandwich, or simply toss it with pasta or rice, it's super-easy to make and great to rely on when there's not a lot of time to prepare a meal.

1. Place the broccoli in a steamer pot over boiling water and cook for 4 minutes, or until just tender.

2. Rinse the broccoli under cold water to stop the cooking. Drain.

3. Transfer the steamed broccoli to a food processor, add the remaining ingredients, and puree.

4. Serve with fish or chicken or stirred into pasta, rice, or quinoa. The pesto can be refrigerated for up to 1 week or frozen for up to 3 months.

big kid guacamole

3 ripe avocados

2 tomatoes, seeded and diced

2 tablespoons finely diced red onion

2 tablespoons chopped fresh cilantro

Juice of ½ lime

¼ teaspoon salt

Avocados are heavenly—creamy, smooth, and delicious. I even use them in sweet recipes like the Avocado Shake (page 260), but if there's one thing I make in our house weekly with them, it's guacamole. Kenya and Chloe once had a bad experience in a Mexican restaurant we frequent often. The guac we normally get (and which my kids are mad for) came out *super*-spicy, loaded with jalapeños, and after their first (and last) bites of it, they were so scarred I was sure they'd never touch the stuff again.

Determined to get them back up and riding on the guacamole bike again, I came up with this Big Kid Guacamole. After many assurances that it was "no spicy" and letting them help me make it, they were happily back to eating the stuff. Whether you're making Black Bean Cakes (page 224), Shrimp Tacos (page 177), or any other Mexican-inspired weelicious recipe, this guacamole will add an extra dimension of flavor and nutrition, and your kids will love it. Holy guacamole!

1. Cut the avocados in half and remove the pits.

2. Scoop the avocado flesh into a bowl and use a wooden spoon or fork to mash the avocados. Allow a few small chunks to remain.

3. Fold in the remaining ingredients until completely incorporated.

4. Serve immediately, or refrigerate for up to 3 days. The top layer will turn brown, but it will stay bright green underneath.

DAWN: Just made this to bring to a friend's place tonight for a kid- and adult-friendly snack . . . it only took 10 minutes and tasted delicious, from what I sampled!

avocado lime sauce

I originally came up with this simple sauce as a dip to accompany my Cheesy Chicken Taquitos (page 178), but one night when I found my husband in front of the fridge eating it straight out of the bowl, I knew I was on to something. Whenever you need a really good sauce or dip to go along with taquitos, tacos, or chips, as a sauce for grilled chicken or fish or even cut-up veggies, try this—it's a little bit different from the usual guacamole. You'll get a lot of mileage out of this one.

1. Place all of the ingredients in a food processor and puree.

2. Serve with taquitos. The sauce will keep in the fridge for 2 to 3 days.

½ cup

1 tablespoon chopped onion or shallot

1 small garlic clove, minced

2 avocados

1 tablespoon chopped fresh cilantro

Juice of ½ lime

Salt to taste

carrot-miso-ginger dressing

2 cups

2 medium carrots, peeled and chopped

2 celery stalks, chopped

1 tablespoon chopped fresh ginger

½ cup cherry tomatoes

1 cucumber, peeled and chopped

2 scallions, chopped

1 tablespoon low-sodium soy sauce

¼ cup rice vinegar

3 tablespoons white or yellow miso

This is a win-win salad dressing for everyone in your family. It's packed with a wide array of vegetables, so you know your kids are getting their vitamins and minerals, and adults will love that the dressing is fresh and delicious-tasting and virtually fat-free. Savory miso provides a rich, thick texture, and rice vinegar and ginger add just the right amount of tang and zip. Let your kids tear up some lettuce while you add a few of their favorite veggies for a dinner starter that will knock their socks off and make *you* feel healthy all over!

1. Place all the ingredients in a food processor and blend until smooth.

2. Serve over salad or as a dip for vegetables. The dressing keeps in the fridge for 3 to 4 days.

ranch dip

When I prepare vegetables for my kids (which is daily), I often use a bit of fun to encourage them to eat more than just one or two bites. I've got lots of veggie methods: I roast them up with a bit of maple syrup, slice them thin and bake up chips, add a sprinkle of zesty herbs, let the kids squirt something yummy on them (such as Bragg Liquid Aminos), or add a delicious dip, such as this one.

When I was a kid, ranch was one of my favorite dressings, but it usually came straight out of a store-bought squeeze bottle, loaded with additives. This version re-creates the great taste and creamy texture I used to love, but it's incredibly fresh and healthy. If you're a parent who's had an uphill battle trying to get your kid to eat veggies, next time your kids are really hungry and want something to munch on, put this dip out with an assortment of cut-up veggies, such as carrots, cucumbers, bell peppers, or sugar snap peas. I find that if I just start eating it on my own (without saying a thing to the kids), they want to mimic me, dipping away and enjoying every last bite!

½ cup

¼ cup plain Greek yogurt (low-fat or full-fat)

2 tablespoons mayonnaise or Vegenaise

1 tablespoon chopped fresh chives

1 teaspoon lemon juice

1 teaspoon Dijon mustard

½ teaspoon garlic powder

½ teaspoon onion powder

Salt to taste

1. Place all the ingredients in a bowl and stir to combine.

2. Serve immediately or refrigerate, covered, for up to 1 week.

ALLISON: I love getting carrots and celery from our CSA box, chopping them up, and putting them in my daughter's laptop lunch box for school with Ranch Dip. She loves dipping the veggies into the dip. The dip is perfect and healthy and helps get her to eat her veggies in her lunch box.

BETSY: I've been trying to reduce the amount of processed foods my family consumes, and I make this Ranch Dip all the time. I pack up a container with dip and a bunch of veggies and we're all set for a healthy snack on the go. We even had a vegetable challenge week—I challenged every member of our family to see who could eat 21 servings of veggies in one week. For some reason, the kids think veggies are for dinner only. None of us would have met our goal without Ranch Dip!

ricotta veggie dip

4 to 6 servings

1 tablespoon vegetable or canola oil

1 small yellow onion, diced

1 small garlic clove, minced

½ cup grated carrot

1 cup grated zucchini

½ teaspoon kosher salt

1 cup ricotta cheese

1 tablespoon fresh lemon juice

ACCOMPANIMENTS

Pita chips, bagel chips, pretzel chips, raw or steamed vegetables

Whenever I'm packing up a school lunch, I always try to think outside the box so my kids will be excited by what's inside. As delicious and versatile as a sandwich can be, it's still fun to switch things up and add something nutritious and out of the ordinary, like this protein- and veggie-packed dip. While the ricotta adds savor and a bit of tang, the dip gets its naturally sweet taste from the caramelized veggies, making it perfect for the lunch box or any time of day. Toss in a few bagel chips and I assure you that your crew will be excited.

1. Heat 1 teaspoon of the oil in a sauté pan over medium heat, add the onion, and sauté for 4 minutes, or until tender.

2. Add the garlic, carrot, zucchini, and salt and sauté for 4 more minutes, or until tender and golden. Set aside to cool.

3. In a medium bowl, combine the ricotta cheese, lemon juice, and cooled vegetables and stir to combine.

4. Serve with your desired accompaniments. The dip will keep for 3 to 4 days in the fridge.

edamame salsa

Given that Americans spend more money on salsa than ketchup, it shouldn't be surprising that it's so popular with kids. I use salsa's appeal to invent different versions using all my kids' favorite foods.

As a mom, I love that this salsa provides a nice hit of protein. And it's delicious. The first time I made it and laid it out with some baked tortilla chips, Chloe bypassed the chip and opted to scoop it into her mouth with a spoon! Mmm, salsa!

1. Place all the ingredients in a bowl and stir until well combined.

2. Serve with tortilla chips. The salsa keeps for 3 to 4 days in the fridge.

TIP: *To save money, buy big bags of frozen edamame, defrost only what you need, and add to recipes like this one or simply eat them on their own!*

2 cups

1 cup shelled cooked edamame beans, chopped

½ cup chopped tomato

¼ cup diced red onion

2 tablespoons chopped fresh cilantro

Juice of 1 lime

¼ teaspoon kosher salt

weelicious tomato sauce

2 cups

1 tablespoon olive oil

½ onion, diced

½ teaspoon salt

1 garlic clove, chopped

½ teaspoon dried Italian herbs

One 15-ounce can tomato sauce

1 teaspoon agave nectar, honey, or sugar

It seems as if we go through gallons of tomato sauce in our house. We use it to make pizza, toss with pasta, top fish and chicken, use as a dip for vegetables, and much more. I like to make homemade sauce using fresh tomatoes from my farmers' market whenever they're in season, but when I can't get my hands on fresh, I use organic canned tomatoes sauce, as in this version. The recipe is really fast and easy and is versatile enough to use in most of your favorite recipes that call for a red sauce. Best of all, you can make it year-round!

1. Heat the oil in a medium saucepan over medium heat, add the onion and salt, and sauté for 5 minutes, or until the onion is softened.

2. Add the garlic and herbs and sauté for 1 minute.

3. Add the tomato sauce and agave, stir to combine, turn the heat to medium-low, and cook for 5 to 10 minutes, until slightly thickened.

4. Serve. The sauce keeps in the fridge for up to 1 week or in the freezer for up to 3 months.

JESS: This is a staple at our house! I made a big batch the other night and froze ice cube tray portions of it. Don't know why I hadn't thought of it before. It's the perfect amount to go on a serving of pasta for my thirteen-month-old! And talk about easy—just pop a cup in the microwave for a few seconds and you're good to go.

JULIE: I just made a double batch of this and it was delicious. I froze half and served half with homemade meatballs. Yum! Much lower in sodium than the jarred sauce I'd been buying, and very quick and easy. Can't wait to make with fresh local tomatoes if this winter ever ends.

raspberr-wee sauce

I like to stock up on frozen berries, primarily because both my kids think they're one of the best breakfasts *and* desserts around. I don't even have to go to the trouble of putting them into a smoothie. The two of them will sit quietly and down half a bag in one shot, their mouths and fingers requiring a major scrubbing afterward to remove the stains. But as much as they love eating frozen berries on their own, they'll always make a beeline for my Raspberr-Wee Sauce. The gorgeous red color is hypnotic, and when Kenya and Chloe first tasted it on some Greek yogurt, they went nuts. Even my husband, who normally likes his yogurt unadorned, adds this sauce until there's more sauce than yogurt in his bowl.

Raspberries are a powerhouse of nutrition, boasting magnesium, vitamin C, and plenty of dietary fiber. Whether you decide to serve this sauce on some protein-packed Greek yogurt, ice cream, waffles, or even on a sandwich with a spread of almond butter or cream cheese, it's a treat that you'll definitely want to become a staple in your fridge.

1½ cups

1 tablespoon cornstarch

One 12-ounce bag frozen raspberries

2 tablespoons honey or agave nectar

1. Whisk the cornstarch and ¼ cup water in a small bowl.

2. Place the raspberries and honey in a medium saucepan over medium-low heat, stirring to combine and mashing the raspberries with the back of a spoon. Bring the mixture to a simmer.

3. Add the cornstarch mixture to the raspberries and stir until the sauce thickens, about 2 minutes.

4. Cool and serve over yogurt, ice cream, pancakes, and more! The sauce can be refrigerated for up to 2 weeks.

fruity avocado dip

Did you know that the avocado is actually a fruit? While they're more commonly found in guacamole and on burgers, I've become a big fan of mashing them and mixing in things like pomegranate seeds and grapes. But you can use almost any in-season fruits you have on hand, so you can enjoy this dip all year long.

1. In a large bowl, mash the avocados with the lemon juice and honey.

2. Fold in the remaining ingredients until combined.

3. Serve immediately.

TIP: *This dip can be made with diced peaches, strawberries, blueberries, pears, or any other seasonal fruit of your choice.*

2 cups

2 avocados, peeled and seeded

1 tablespoon lemon juice

2 teaspoons honey

1 tablespoon chopped fresh mint

¼ cup pomegranate seeds

¼ cup diced mango

¼ cup quartered grapes

ACCOMPANIMENTS

Apple slices, pear slices, banana chunks, or plantain chips

snacks

graham crackers

makes a *lot*,
depending on the
shape and size
you cut them in

1 cup whole wheat flour

**1½ cups all-purpose
flour**

**½ cup packed dark
brown sugar**

½ teaspoon salt

**1 teaspoon ground
cinnamon**

1 teaspoon baking soda

**1 stick (½ cup) unsalted
butter, chilled and
cubed**

¼ cup honey

I don't make *everything* our family eats from scratch, but I do try to make as many of the sweet treats my kids consume as possible. Some time ago, I realized that Kenya had never eaten a graham cracker. I think he was just over three at the time. How was that possible?! Graham crackers are a total cookie rite of passage for kids! I think I ate them starting from the time I could chew, so, on that fateful day when I saw Kenya looking quizzically as his friends ate out of a box of graham crackers, a new recipe challenge was born for me.

It's not that I'm against prepackaged cookies or crackers, but it's so much more fun to make them with your kids, and I feel a lot better about putting a sweet treat in my kids' school lunch when it's homemade. Not only does this graham cracker recipe make a *ton* of cookies, but you can cut them out and freeze them to bake as you need them later on. It takes no time for me to make the dough, roll it out, and then let the kids take over, using mini cookie cutters to pop out the sweetest, crispest graham crackers I've ever tasted. They remind me of the ones I used to eat as a kid, but even better!

You can't mess these up by under- or overbaking them—the dough is unbelievably forgiving.

DEBRA: These graham crackers are one of the first recipes I made with my son. He had such a blast helping measure and pour everything, then I let him pick which shapes he wanted to use with the cookie cutters. It was a great first and has led to many more kitchen adventures!

1. Preheat the oven to 350°F.

2. In a food processor or standing mixer, combine the flours, brown sugar, salt, cinnamon, and baking soda.

3. Add the chilled butter to the mixture and pulse/mix until the mixture resembles coarse meal.

4. Add the honey and ¼ cup water and continue to mix until well combined.

5. Remove the dough, shape it into a flat disk, and place it between two large pieces of parchment paper.

6. Roll out the dough ¼ inch thick. Cut into crackers or shapes.

7. Place the crackers on a Silpat or parchment-lined baking sheet and bake for 15 minutes. They're a little soft when they come out of the oven, but they firm up nicely.

8. Cool and serve. Store, covered, on the counter for up to 1 week or up to 2 weeks in the fridge.

TO FREEZE: *After step 6, place the cutout cookie shapes onto a baking sheet and freeze for 20 minutes. Remove, place in a zip-top bag, label, and freeze for up to 4 months. When you're ready to bake the crackers, jump back to step 7, allowing 1 or 2 minutes more baking time.*

TIP: *A delicious variation is to substitute 1 cup oat bran for the whole wheat flour and increase the all-purpose flour to 2 cups.*

KARA: My mother-in-law got me a set of letter and number cookie cutters, and in one homeschooling lesson we can cover so much with this recipe—measuring, nutrition, motor skills, and then a healthy snack that lets us practice spelling and math!

apple-cinnamon sticks

about 30 sticks

1 cup all-purpose flour

½ teaspoon baking powder

2 tablespoons packed brown sugar

2 tablespoons wheat germ

¾ teaspoon ground cinnamon

½ cup peeled grated apple

2 tablespoons canola or vegetable oil

There are hundreds of brands of boxed cookies and crackers on the marketplace, but whenever I'm at the supermarket and look at the side of the packaging to read the ingredient list, I can't pronounce half of the things I see. It's all the inspiration I need to want to rush home and create something homemade.

These apple-cinnamon sticks are crisp and sweet, better than (and probably unlike) anything you could buy at the grocery. They're great for anything from breakfast, to a snack, to put in your kid's lunch box, or even to enjoy as a healthy and sweet dessert treat.

1. Preheat the oven to 400°F.

2. Place the flour, baking powder, brown sugar, wheat germ, and cinnamon in a bowl and stir to combine.

3. Add the grated apple to the flour mixture and, using your hands, toss to coat the shredded apple.

4. Add the oil and continue to work with your hands until a dough comes together. This will take 2 to 3 minutes; keep working until the dough is smooth.

5. Shape the apple-cinnamon dough into a flat rectangular disk and let it rest for 1 to 2 minutes. Roll out the dough ½ inch thick on parchment paper or a clean, dry surface.

6. Using a knife, cut the dough into sticks—2 inches long by ¼ inch wide— or cut out shapes with a small cookie cutter.

7. Bake the sticks on a Silpat or parchment-lined cookie sheet for 20 minutes, or until golden.

8. Cool and serve. The sticks will keep for 3 to 4 days on the counter, covered.

whole wheat seed crackers

makes a *lot*,
depending on the
shape and size
you cut them in

½ cup whole wheat flour

1 cup all-purpose flour

½ teaspoon onion powder

½ teaspoon salt

4 tablespoons (½ stick) unsalted butter, chilled and cubed

1 teaspoon fennel seeds

1 teaspoon chia seeds

1 teaspoon flax seeds

1 teaspoon poppy seeds

Baking for others during the holidays is a tradition I enjoy, and this past year I decided to make something for my friends and my kids' teachers that's scrumptious but a little bit on the lighter side. These Whole Wheat Seed Crackers have that home-baked feel, are crisp and flavorful, and are even pretty to look at. I feel better knowing that I'm giving people something a bit more healthy that's still perfect for the holidays. And I promise you they have fewer calories than a Yule log!

1. Preheat the oven to 400°F.

2. Place the flours, onion powder, and salt in a food processor and pulse to combine.

3. Add the chilled butter and pulse until it resembles coarse meal.

4. Add ⅓ cup water and pulse until the dough comes together into a ball.

5. Remove the dough, shape it into a flat disk, and place it between two pieces of parchment paper.

6. Roll out the dough to ¼ inch thick, lift the top sheet of parchment, and sprinkle the seeds on top of the dough. Put the parchment paper back on top and roll out the dough a bit more, to press the seeds into it. Remove the paper and cut the dough into crackers or ½-inch by 2-inch sticks, or use cookie cutters to make it into shapes.

7. Place the crackers on a parchment-lined baking sheet and bake for 18 to 20 minutes, until firm.

8. Cool and serve. The crackers keep for up to 1 week.

TO FREEZE: *After step 6, place the cutout shapes onto a baking sheet and freeze for 20 minutes. Remove, place in a zip-top bag, label, and freeze for up to 4 months. When you're ready to bake the crackers, jump back to step 7, allowing 1 to 2 minutes more baking time.*

sunflower seed brittle

My grandparents always used to give us peanut brittle. I'd munch bite after bite to get that sweet, caramelized nutty taste. Because so many schools are nut-free these days, I thought I'd try making brittle with sunflower seeds so that Kenya could take it to lunch. And instead of using high fructose corn syrup, I swapped in brown rice syrup. I ended up liking this brittle even more than my grandparents' classic version!

1. Preheat the oven to 375°F and lay parchment paper on a baking sheet.

2. In a medium bowl, combine the butter, brown rice syrup, and honey.

3. Add the sunflower seeds and stir until they're coated evenly. Spread the mixture on the parchment.

4. Bake for 10 to 12 minutes, or until golden.

5. Set the brittle aside to cool thoroughly, then break it into pieces. The brittle will keep for a week or more in a covered container on the counter.

6. Serve alone or with ice cream for a treat!

serves 4

1 tablespoon unsalted butter, melted

2 tablespoons brown rice syrup

1 tablespoon honey

1 cup hulled raw sunflower seeds

banana peanut butter muffins

30 to 35 mini muffins

1 cup all-purpose flour

¾ cup whole wheat flour

½ teaspoon salt

2 teaspoons baking powder

2 medium ripe bananas, mashed

1 large egg, beaten

⅓ cup sugar

⅓ cup vegetable or canola oil

½ cup milk

Creamy peanut or almond butter

Jam or jelly, for topping (optional)

This recipe makes me *really* happy. I've always been one of those people who loves finding a chunk or swirl of something delicious inside my ice cream, a donut, or even a muffin. One day I decided that there would be nothing better than finding a big swirl of peanut butter inside of a banana muffin, so I got to work. The combination of bananas and peanut butter is a classic, and they make for a great marriage in these muffins. My husband, who loves putting his own stamp on some of the recipes I cook, had the idea to spread some strawberry preserves on top of his to make a banana PB&J muffin. It was delicious!

1. Preheat the oven to 400°F and grease a pan of mini muffin cups.

2. Combine the flours, salt, and baking powder in a medium bowl and mix together.

3. In another bowl, mash the bananas. Add the egg and sugar and stir to combine. Add the oil and milk and mix until smooth.

4. Slowly add the dry ingredients to the wet ingredients and combine, taking care not to overmix the batter.

5. Using a small ice cream scoop, drop 1 tablespoon of batter into each mini muffin cup and top with ½ teaspoon of peanut butter. Place another 1 teaspoon of batter on top of the peanut butter to cover.

6. Bake for 13 minutes, or until dry on top. (If you choose to use regular muffin cups, bake for 20 minutes.) This makes 12 to 14 regular-sized muffins.

7. Cool and serve. Spread a little jam or jelly on top just before serving for a real treat. These muffins keep for about 1 day, covered, on the counter or up to 4 days refrigerated.

parsnip muffins

12 muffins

1 cup all-purpose flour

½ cup whole wheat flour

1 teaspoon baking powder

¾ teaspoon baking soda

½ teaspoon salt

¼ teaspoon ground nutmeg

½ teaspoon ground cinnamon

3 large eggs

½ cup packed brown sugar

½ cup plain Greek yogurt

¼ cup vegetable oil

2 teaspoons pure vanilla extract

2 parsnips, peeled and grated (about 1 cup)

CREAM CHEESE FILLING

One 8-ounce package cream cheese, softened

1 teaspoon pure vanilla extract

3 tablespoons packed brown sugar

Poor parsnips, they get no love. They're rarely found on restaurant menus and probably not in your home kitchen either. Whatever your feelings about parsnips, these muffins will make you want to see a lot more of them.

Parsnips are a sweet root vegetable, similar in appearance to carrots but creamy in color. When cooked, they have a sweet, rich flavor that provides the base for these yummy muffins. My husband took a batch to my daughter's playgroup and moms kept coming up to him to rave about the taste. They were amazed when he said the muffins were made with parsnips.

While the presence of parsnip may not produce as much wonder from your kids, they will certainly get a pleasant surprise of their own when they take a bite and find a smooth center full of sweet cream cheese.

1. Preheat the oven to 375°F and grease or line a pan of muffin cups.

2. Combine the flours, baking powder, baking soda, salt, nutmeg, and cinnamon in a large bowl and whisk to combine.

3. In a separate large bowl, whisk the eggs. Add the brown sugar, yogurt, oil, and vanilla and stir to combine.

4. Stir the grated parsnips into the flour mixture to coat.

5. Add the dry ingredients to the wet and stir until just combined.

6. To make the cream cheese filling, place all the ingredients in a bowl and whisk until smooth (it's okay if there are a few lumps).

7. Fill each muffin cup one third of the way with batter and top with 1 tablespoon of the cream cheese filling. Drop another tablespoon of the batter on top of the cream cheese mixture and then top with an additional tablespoon of the cream cheese filling.

8. Bake for 20 to 25 minutes, until golden.

9. Cool and serve. These muffins keep for about 1 day, covered, on the counter or up to 4 days refrigerated.

banana wee-eat germ muffins

about 36
mini muffins

1 cup all-purpose flour

1 cup wheat germ

1 teaspoon baking soda

½ teaspoon baking powder

1 teaspoon salt

3 very ripe medium bananas, mashed, plus 2 bananas for topping

½ cup honey or agave nectar

3 tablespoons vegetable or canola oil

1 tablespoon pure vanilla extract

1 large egg

This recipe is going to blow your mind (and your taste buds)! I've been making banana bread for years, but I must admit my original recipe contained pretty significant quantities of butter and sugar. Those days are long gone for me, but I still crave banana bread and wanted to try out a much healthier version for my family. Not to brag, but my original recipe was pretty fantastic, so I had to keep testing and experimenting to try to match the original's flavor and texture. I also decided to make muffins instead of a loaf, as portion control is easier to maintain and mini muffins are the perfect size for little hands.

I love cooking with wheat germ because it contains 23 nutrients (including potassium and riboflavin)—more per ounce than any other grain or vegetable—and has protein and a high concentration of complex carbohydrates. It turned out to be a great addition to this recipe, as it adds great flavor, too.

I was shocked at how light and sweet the new recipe turned out. When you try it, remember that the key is using super-ripe bananas. Our grocery puts the brown, spotty ones on sale several times a week, so I always grab a bunch for recipes just like this! Keep super-ripe bananas in the fridge for a few days and you'll be able to use them longer.

1. Preheat the oven to 350°F and grease or line a pan of mini muffin cups.

2. Whisk the flour, wheat germ, baking soda, baking powder, and salt in a medium bowl.

3. In a standing mixer, combine the mashed bananas, honey, oil, vanilla, and egg. Beat until combined.

4. Slowly add the dry ingredients to the wet ingredients until just combined. Do not overmix.

5. Cut the 2 remaining bananas into ¼-inch slices. Fill the muffin cups three-quarters full with the batter and top each with a banana slice.

6. Bake for 15 minutes, or until a toothpick comes out clean. (If you use a regular muffin pan, bake for 20 minutes; this makes 12-regular sized muffins.)

7. Cool and serve. The muffins stay fresh, covered, on the counter for 2 days or in the fridge for 5 to 6 days.

MELANIE: Wow, these are delicious! I am a big believer in wheat germ and am impressed that the recipe called for so much of it.

SONDRA: My thirteen-month-old twins love these—they ate three each as soon as they were cool enough. They could hardly wait—the smell was driving them crazy!

ELITA: These just came out of the oven, and they rock! Another winner. I can't believe how sweet and delicious they are, with just ½ cup of honey and no butter!

TRACY: Made this in a bread loaf pan and it was delicious—my fourteen-month-old ate almost half the loaf for breakfast! Thank you for such a healthy recipe.

MELINDA: So delicious! My little man loved it even more than the normal, butter-laden muffins that I usually make. These freeze *great*. I doubled the recipe and baked these, then froze them so that I could reheat them for breakfast whenever I needed.

sweet potato muffins

Often my kids will come into the kitchen while I'm cooking and yell, "I want to help!" I try to come up with fun ways to get them involved in whatever I'm doing.

Step one is always washing hands, a rule in our kitchen that at times can lead to a battle, but I never give in. Once, when I was making these muffins, Chloe was defiantly insisting on helping me—her seriously filthy mitts clutching an equally dirty whisk. I explained to Chloe that if she washed her hands she could mix all the ingredients in the bowl together *with her hands.* That did the trick. Right to the sink Chloe went to lather up. Plunging her hands into the sweet potato mixture was a fun sensory exercise, and she had a blast, but eating the final result was even better.

1. Preheat the oven to 350°F and grease a pan of mini muffin cups.

2. Place the flour, oats, sweet potato, brown sugar, baking powder, baking soda, salt, and cinnamon in a large bowl and combine, making sure the sweet potato is evenly coated with the mixture.

3. In a separate bowl, whisk the eggs, milk, oil, and vanilla until combined.

4. Slowly combine the dry ingredients with the wet ingredients, taking care not to overmix the batter.

5. Place 1 heaping tablespoon of batter in each mini muffin cup (to fill each two thirds full) and bake for 15 minutes, or until a toothpick inserted comes out clean.

6. Cool and serve with honey, maple syrup, or butter. These muffins will keep for about 1 day, covered, on the counter or for up to 4 or 5 days in the refrigerator.

about 30 mini muffins

1 cup all-purpose flour

1 cup old-fashioned oats (not instant and not steel-cut)

1 cup peeled, grated sweet potato

½ cup packed brown sugar

1 teaspoon baking powder

½ teaspoon baking soda

½ teaspoon salt

1 teaspoon ground cinnamon

2 large eggs

½ cup milk

¼ cup vegetable or canola oil

1 teaspoon pure vanilla extract

ACCOMPANIMENTS

Honey, maple syrup, or butter

apple oat bars

32 squares

¾ cup old-fashioned oats (not instant and not steel-cut)

1 cup pitted Medjool dates (if the dates are very dry, soak them in warm water for a few minutes to soften them)

1½ cups dried apple rings

1 teaspoon ground cinnamon

I have a terrible habit of buying foods the kids love but forgetting that I already have three packages of the same thing at home. Case in point: the *bags* of dried apple rings piled up in my pantry. There I was with four bags of dried apple rings and in need of a tasty snack for munching on. What could be easier than this healthy and delicious four-ingredient recipe? I know, eating them!

1. Place the oats in a food processor and pulse for 30 seconds, or until ground (it's okay if a few small pieces remain).

2. Set aside ¼ cup of the ground oats in a small bowl. Place the remaining ingredients in the food processor and pulse to combine for about 2 minutes, until a ball starts to form.

3. Line a loaf pan (about 8½ x 4½ inches) with plastic wrap. Press the mixture down to mold it into the shape of the pan. Remove the block from the pan and place on a cutting board.

4. Cut the block into 1-inch squares and roll the squares in the reserved ground oats until the squares are evenly coated.

5. Serve. The bars will keep for 1 week on the counter, covered, or in the fridge for 2 weeks.

pbrb "waffle" sammies

4 servings

1 ripe banana

½ cup fresh raspberries

8 slices whole wheat bread

½ cup peanut, almond, or sunflower butter

We love our waffle iron. It's nothing fancy, but it does the job and we use it a lot. You may think having a waffle iron isn't worth it because they're only good for making, well, waffles, but there are a few other things you can do with it. One day when I was making lunch for the kids, the waffle iron was still sitting out from breakfast, and a lightbulb went on in my head. Why not turn my waffle iron into a waffle iron/sandwich press?

Kenya and Chloe were completely taken with the novelty of their "waffle sandwiches." Filled with a beautiful, sweet pinkish puree of raspberries and banana, this is my version of a totally jazzed-up PB&J from my new *multipurpose* waffle iron!

1. Preheat the waffle iron.

2. Place the banana and raspberries in a bowl and mash with a fork.

3. Spread 2 tablespoons of the banana-raspberry mixture on 1 bread slice. Spread 2 tablespoons of nut butter on a second bread slice and press together to make a sandwich. Repeat to make the rest of the sandwiches.

4. Bake each sammie in the waffle iron for 3 minutes, or until golden.

5. Cool and serve.

cinnamon-honey popcorn

I'm a big popcorn eater, so my kids come by their love of it it honestly. The caramel corn you buy in a store can be delicious, but it's usually loaded with sugar and corn syrup. I make my own and let the kids get in on the fun by squeezing on a bit of honey and sprinkling a dash of cinnamon to make this treat something truly special and so much more an enjoyable experience for everyone than just ripping open a box from the store. You can even drop a little surprise toy or treat in the bottom of the bowl to relive your childhood caramel corn memories.

4 servings

1 tablespoon vegetable or canola oil

½ cup unpopped popcorn

1 tablespoon honey

½ teaspoon ground cinnamon

1. Heat a large, heavy pot with a lid and handle over medium-high heat and coat the bottom with the oil.

2. Place the popcorn inside the pot, close the lid, and shake the pot continuously until you no longer hear the corn popping, 4 to 5 minutes.

3. Remove the pot from the heat and drizzle the popcorn with the honey. Sprinkle with the cinnamon and toss to coat evenly.

4. Serve immediately.

chewy granola balls

about 30 balls

½ cup peanut or almond butter

½ cup brown rice syrup

1 cup crispy rice cereal

1½ cups Fruit and Seed Granola (page 85), or your favorite store brand

¼ cup chopped dried fruit: cranberries, cherries, blueberries, raisins, or a combination

One of the greatest challenges when it comes to making kids' snacks or desserts is coming up with recipes that are actually both healthy and something kids *want* to eat. As a parent, you want your kids' food to have nutritional value, but you know it also has to have eye and taste appeal. From the moment Kenya tried these Chewy Granola Balls, I knew I'd fulfilled both criteria.

Loaded with whole grains, protein, and fruit, these granola balls have just the right amount of sweetness and a crunchy, chewy texture that kids seem to love. I brought a batch of them to my informal "focus groups" made up of Kenya's schoolmates and playgroups, and I never had enough to fulfill the demand for seconds. When the crowd is happy, so is Mommy!

1. Place the nut butter and brown rice syrup in a small saucepan and cook over medium-low heat for about 2 minutes, or until it's warm, smooth, and combined.

2. Place the cereal, granola, and fruit in a bowl and stir to combine.

MELISSA: We make these granola balls all the time! They were the first thing to go at my son's second birthday party, and his twenty-five-year-old uncle has specially requested his own batch.

SARAH: My two-year-old loves to help mix these together. They're fast and easy to make, taste great, and are a treat that I feel good about giving him.

3. Pour the warm nut butter mixture into the bowl with the granola mixture and stir to combine.

4. Roll the mixture into 1-inch balls. (I use a mini ice cream scooper to scoop out each portion, but you could also use a tablespoon.)

5. Serve. The granola balls will keep on the counter, covered, for up to 1 week.

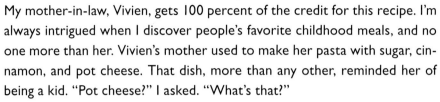

sweet noodles

4 to 6 servings

1 pound rotini noodles

1¼ cups ricotta cheese

¼ cup honey

½ teaspoon ground cinnamon

My mother-in-law, Vivien, gets 100 percent of the credit for this recipe. I'm always intrigued when I discover people's favorite childhood meals, and no one more than her. Vivien's mother used to make her pasta with sugar, cinnamon, and pot cheese. That dish, more than any other, reminded her of being a kid. "Pot cheese?" I asked. "What's that?"

In trying to re-create this dish to experience with my family, the mysterious pot cheese created a problem. I'd never heard of, let alone knew where to get some. I learned that pot cheese has a consistency comparable to ricotta. Since ricotta is much easier to find than pot cheese (believe me, I really tried), that's what I substituted to make this scrumptious treat.

I've never seen my kids eat anything so fast. And because it was pasta, something they normally don't eat sweet, they were all the more fascinated. I thought to myself, are these sweet noodles a breakfast? Snack? Dessert? Side dish? I guess they could work as all of the above, but Kenya and Chloe couldn't care less as long as there's plenty for their little bellies to enjoy.

1. Cook the pasta according to the package directions.

2. In a bowl, mix the ricotta, honey, and cinnamon until creamy.

3. Pour the ricotta mixture over the drained pasta, stir to coat the pasta, and serve.

date-nut bites

We're big fans of dates in our house. We buy a big bag of them every week at the farmers' market. They're my kids' version of candy because they're so sweet, chewy, and rich. If you put them in some cool packaging, they could easily pass in a candy store!

Although the dates we get are perfect on their own, I decided to take them a step further and make healthy "candy" bites out of them. The recipe takes just minutes, and the bites freeze beautifully, too. Well, unless you're making them for Kenya and Chloe, of course. In that case, these treats don't stand a chance of making it to the freezer. Kenya figured out where I'd hid my freshly made batch, carried his little chair over to the counter, opened the tin, and grabbed several handfuls for himself and Chloe. Thank goodness they're made with nature's sugar!

about 65 balls

1 pound Medjool dates, pitted

½ cup shelled walnuts

1 cup unsweetened coconut flakes

1. Puree the dates and walnuts in a food processor until smooth.

2. Place the coconut flakes on a plate.

3. Scoop 1 teaspoon of the date-walnut mixture and roll it into a ball. Repeat with the rest of the mixture. (Or if you want to make the mixture into cute little 1-inch logs, the recipe will yield about 30.)

4. Roll the balls in the coconut flakes to coat.

5. Serve. These keep up to 1 week on the counter, covered, or in the fridge for up to 2 weeks, or up to 3 months frozen.

JOY: I wasn't sure how my eighteen-month-old would react to these, but he immediately asked for more. Now I have to make sure to give him just one at a time, because he'll stuff them into his mouth until he can't fit any more!

TIP: *For a real treat, freeze some of the bites in a zip-top freezer bag and enjoy them frozen!*

strawberry ice pops

about 6 ice pops, depending on the size of your molds

2 ¼ cups strawberries, stems removed

1 tablespoon lemon juice

1 tablespoon honey, agave nectar, or sugar (optional, if your strawberries are on the tart side)

I scream, you scream, we all scream for . . . ice pops! Okay, fine, I know that's not how the song goes, but I promise you'll have some seriously happy little ones after serving this treat.

Why do ice pop recipes tend to have so much sugar in them? Not only is all that sugar bad for you, but the ice pops lose all the naturally sweet taste of the fruit. I think this recipe produces a pop that's totally superior to sugar-added store brands. Not only do these pops have a bright rich strawberry flavor, but they're a good bargain, too. This recipe makes twelve ice pops for a fraction of the price you'd pay for a box of six "healthy" or organic pops.

I serve these to kids when they come to our house in the summertime, and you should see their eyes light up when I pull them out. The best part is always after they eat them, when the little ones aren't jacked up on sugar and the mommies and daddies are *very* happy!

KELTIE: These ice pops are so easy to make and taste better than the ones you buy in the store. When my son asks if he can have an ice pop for breakfast, I can say yes knowing that he's getting something nutritious and not full of refined sugars. My son actually lost his first tooth while eating one.

1. Combine all the ingredients in a food processor or blender and puree.

2. Pour the mixture into ice pop molds and freeze for at least 4 hours and up to 4 weeks.

3. Unmold and serve.

TIP: *If you can find them, I recommend investing in ice pop molds that are BPA free. Ice pop molds can differ in size, so if you have any extra mixture, enjoy it as a smoothie.*

banana cream ice pops

When my husband first heard the name of this recipe (I originally called it Banana Cream Cheese Ice Pops), he made a face (not a good one) and said, "Well, that sounds disgusting." You'd think trying to feed two children would be enough. He's the reason I occasionally tell people I have three kids. Well, he did an about-face upon tasting one of these pops and basically begged me to let him package them and sell them. Ah, children.

1. Combine all the ingredients in a food processor or blender and puree.

2. Pour the mixture into ice pop molds and freeze for at least 6 hours and up to 4 weeks.

3. Unmold and serve.

8 ice pops

2 bananas

1 teaspoon pure vanilla extract

4 ounces cream cheese

1 cup milk

2 tablespoons honey

coconut-pineapple pops

8 ice pops

One 14-ounce can low-fat or regular coconut milk

2 cups chopped pineapple

2 tablespoons honey

You'd think I was raising two Eskimos. Even in the depths of winter, Kenya and Chloe ask me for ice pops. While I'm shivering in the corner of the kitchen, watching them lick these creamy coconut pops adorned with tiny pieces of fresh pineapple, they're happy and smiling, enjoying every last drop.

1. Combine all the ingredients in a food processor or blender and puree.

2. Pour the mixture into ice pop molds and freeze for at least 6 hours and up to 4 weeks.

3. Unmold and serve.

KIM: I discovered weelicious when I was looking for new recipes for my picky two-year-old son. I loved the video of you and Kenya making Coconut-Pineapple Pops together, so I followed what you did and let my son, Coen, help. It was such a yummy, positive experience, and he's now interested in trying different foods, especially when he helps cook! It's really changed his attitude toward food, and we now share something special, cooking. Thank you!

TIP: *For fun, dice any remaining pineapple into tiny cubes, toss them into the ice pop molds, and top with the coconut mixture, so that there are pineapple chunks in the pops!*

mango pops

I believe our responsibility to make sure we give our kids healthy foods free of additives and chemicals that are potentially going to be toxic in their bodies—like artificial food dyes. The challenge for us parents is that kids respond strongly to bright colors, and so many unhealthy foods on the marketplace target our children by dyeing their products in hues that can only be created in a lab. I'm not saying that it's easy, but avoiding food colors and dyes can be less complicated than you think.

My kids love ice pops (what kid doesn't), so one simple thing I do is make these vivid Mango Pops. Not only are they a vibrant orange-yellow that's totally natural and rivals any artificially colored ice pop, they're also sweet, delicious, and perfect during the summer heat, or any time of year for that matter. Plus, my kids enjoy making them almost as much as they love eating them.

Instead of buying a box of ice pops made with additives that you probably can't even pronounce, have your kids help you whip up a batch of these Mango Pops. You'll know you're doing their bodies good and give yourself some peace of mind. Color yourself impressed!

8 ice pops

2 mangoes, peeled, pitted, and chopped

1 cup rice or almond milk, or any milk you like

2 tablespoons honey

1. Combine all the ingredients in a food processor or blender and puree.

2. Pour the mixture into ice pop molds and freeze for at least 6 hours and up to 4 weeks.

3. Unmold and serve.

pea pops

8 servings

**One 16-ounce bag
frozen peas**

When I first had this recipe recommended to me, I was appalled—it sounded so gross! But I'm never one to shy away from giving an idea a whirl, so I decided to whip up a batch of my own.

I wasn't exactly sure how my kids would react when they first saw green peas in ice pop form, and I didn't have huge expectations. But I guess the mere idea of peas on a stick was hilarious to them, because they were fascinated, as many of their friends have been when they've come over and tried them. Just goes to show that you can't impose your own thoughts on what you think your kids will and won't like.

For all the parents out there who can't get their little ones to try a green vegetable, give these a try!

1. Fill each ice pop mold with about ¼ cup frozen peas. You want the peas to go almost to the top of the mold.

2. Cover with cold water and place sticks in the molds. Freeze for at least 4 hours and up to 4 weeks.

3. Unmold and serve.

tropical fruit salad

Several years ago, we went on a family vacation to Hawaii. I arrived with dreams of making all sorts of exotic dishes full of new and interesting ingredients. Kenya and I loved walking around the markets sipping coconut water right out of whole coconuts and salivating over the sweetest, juiciest, and ripest mangoes, papayas, passion fruit, limes, and "apple" bananas (a smaller, more dense banana that has a faint taste of, you guessed it, apple) and unusual fruits and veggies such as jackfruit and breadfruit. It was awesome, especially for a farmers' market geek like me!

After we returned home I started buying passion fruit from our local farmers' market and even planted a passion fruit vine in our yard that produces a hundred at a time. But they're also quite easy to find in most groceries. Just look for a round, shriveled, bright yellow or purple fruit (if it's shriveled, you know it's ripe). When you cut into it, passion fruit reveals its sweet, tangy juice with little edible seeds that are packed with vitamin A, potassium, and fiber. Kenya and Chloe like to eat the seeds straight out of the shell, but they're also great sprinkled on yogurt or added to something like this fruit salad, which contains mangoes and papayas, both rich in beta-carotene and, along with pineapple, bursting with vitamin C. And by the way, the lime or lemon juice makes this tropical fruit salad truly extraordinary tasting.

1. In a large bowl, combine the mango, papaya, banana, and pineapple.

2. Sprinkle the lime juice, passion fruit juice, and passion fruit seeds all over the fruit salad, toss to combine, and serve.

TIP: *Spoon over yogurt, ice cream, or sorbet for a special treat!*

---

4 servings

1 cup peeled, pitted, and cubed mango

1 cup peeled, seeded, and cubed papaya

1 banana, peeled and sliced

1 cup peeled, cored, and cubed pineapple

2 tablespoons lime or lemon juice

Juice and seeds from ½ passion fruit

strawberry fruit leather

8 long strips

3 cups washed, stemmed strawberries

1 tablespoon honey

My kids love fruit roll-ups, and while there are some great brands out there made with just fruit, I know I can save a ton of dough making them myself. While I didn't have to spend a lot of money trying to figure out how to make them, I have spent a lot of time! In an effort to perfect the recipe, I made fifteen (yes, fifteen!) batches of strawberry leather. It was a frustrating challenge to say the least, especially when making fruit leather seems so easy in principle. It's just fruit and heat, right? Well, kind of. Timing, oven type, and berry quality all have to be taken into consideration.

Knowing that people could have varying results with my recipe, I asked friends and a bunch of weelicious readers to test it on their own. Everyone's outcomes were slightly different, so although I can give guidelines here, you'll have to experiment with the cooking time. My advice is to spread the mixture as evenly as possible on the baking sheet and keep a close eye on the fruit while it's cooking. Be prepared for a bit of trial and error, but don't lose your cool. Hopefully when you find your ideal cooking time, you'll be knocking out batches of your own fruit leather with ease.

If you have a dehydrator, you'll be thrilled with the results of this recipe. Just see the slightly different method below.

KIMAREE: My kids love this fruit leather! The other day my neighbor offered my daughter commercially made fruit leather and she told him, "No, thank you. We make our own and they are much healthier!"

1. Preheat the oven to 250°F and line a large baking sheet with parchment paper.

2. Place the strawberries and honey in a blender and puree until smooth.

3. Pour the mixture onto the baking sheet and spread it into a large rectangle with the back of a spoon or spatula (my rectangle was 11 x 15 inches), *making sure that the mixture is spread completely even.*

4. Bake for 2 to 3 hours, until the fruit leather is dry and not sticky to the touch. Remember, cooking times will vary depending on how thick you spread your mixture and how

much water (juice) is naturally in the fruit. Also, every oven is different, so the cooking time may be less than 2 hours if your oven tends to be hot.

5. Allow the fruit leather to sit and cool to room temperature. It takes several hours for the fruit to soften up; when you first take the leather out of the oven the edges will be a bit dry and crisp, but if you allow it to sit overnight it softens up nicely. I like to roll it up and place it in a covered container.

6. Use a knife, pizza cutter, or kitchen shears to cut the fruit leather into 8 long strips, keeping the paper on the back. Roll the leather into "roll-ups."

7. The fruit leather will keep for at least a month in a covered container.

TIP: *You could use a Silpat instead of parchment paper, but obviously you won't have a convenient paper backing.*

IF USING A DEHYDRATOR: *After step 2, pour the mixture on a lined dehydrator sheet and dehydrate the fruit leather at 135°F for 5 to 6 hours.*

dinner

chicken on a stick

8 sticks

2 cups cornflakes, whole wheat flakes, or other flaky cereal

1 teaspoon kosher salt

1 cup buttermilk (or 1 scant cup milk plus 1 teaspoon white vinegar or lemon juice)

1 pound chicken tenders, cleaned

1 package ice pop sticks

Vegetable or canola oil spray

Ranch Dip (page 113), for serving

Kids love anything on a stick. Or so I've found. I never would have believed it before Kenya started eating solids, but it's true. Ice pops, corn dogs, shish kebabs . . . put whatever you're making on a stick and watch what happens! It just makes eating so much more enjoyable for kids.

For this chicken-on-a-stick recipe, I added a dipping sauce to increase the fun factor! Even better is that this recipe is totally healthy. When I unveiled these to some of Kenya and Chloe's friends, the kids were all yelling, "I want a chicken stick!" The funniest part was watching the parents craving some for themselves but assuming it wasn't good for their waistline. Not this version! It's low in fat and high in protein and fiber, especially if you use a wholesome cereal for the coating. Plus, they're baked, not fried, so you still get the great taste and crunch without the grease.

The next time you want a super-easy recipe for a party with kids and their parents or even just for family dinner, make this recipe and you'll have tons of happy tummies!

ROSIE: **When my daughter first started eating solids, she refused to touch chicken, so she got frustrated (she had yet to master the fork). I discovered your Chicken on a Stick recipe, and she loved it—she was able to grab and bite it for herself. She's two now, and it's her favorite thing to eat.**

1. Preheat the oven to 375°F and grease a large baking sheet.

2. Place the cereal and salt in a zip-top bag and crush the flakes with a rolling pin. Or you can use a food processor and pulse until the mixture resembles bread crumbs.

3. Pour the buttermilk in one bowl and the cereal coating in another.

4. Skewer the chicken tenders lengthwise onto the ice pop sticks, leaving a 1-inch handle sticking out.

5. Place the chicken tenders in the buttermilk, then roll them in the cereal, coating the chicken completely.

6. Place the chicken tender sticks on the baking sheet, lightly spray them with oil, and cover the stick handles with a bit of foil to keep them from burning.

7. Bake for 16 to 18 minutes, until cooked through.

8. Serve with Ranch Dip.

TO FREEZE: *After step 5, place the chicken tenders on a baking sheet and freeze for 30 minutes. Transfer to a zip-top bag, label, and freeze for up to 4 months. To bake, do not defrost; just add 3 to 5 minutes to the baking time.*

mexican enchiladas

8 servings

1 tablespoon olive oil

1 small yellow onion, chopped (about 1 cup)

1 red bell pepper, diced

1 teaspoon kosher salt

1 teaspoon ground cumin

1 small garlic clove, minced

1 pound chicken breasts, cooked and shredded

1 cup frozen corn, defrosted

1½ cups shredded Mexican cheese blend

One 28-ounce can enchilada sauce

8 flour tortillas

OPTIONAL GARNISHES

Chopped cilantro, sour cream, queso fresco

"Why don't you come over for dinner with the kids tonight!" At least once a week, my enthusiasm gets ahead of practical concerns and I invite one of my mom friends over for a weeknight dinner. That is followed immediately by the thought, *Who am I kidding? When am I going to have time to prepare dinner for four kids and four adults when I've already got a crazy day of work ahead of me?* As a result of my big mouth and boundless naive optimism, I've forced myself to become the (self-proclaimed) queen of doubling recipes and freezing the surplus for these types of occasions. And these enchiladas are the perfect candidate for doing just that. Whether you're cooking for two or twelve, there's nothing easier than pulling these out of the freezer, popping them into the oven, and, thirty minutes later, enjoying warm tortillas filled with chicken, veggies, and tons of gooey cheese.

At my last impromptu dinner, we were all sitting around, chowing down on this Mexican treat, when my friend leaned in to me to say, "I can't believe you had the time to make these!" I didn't have the heart to keep my secret from her. When it's really that easy, why not have friends over every night?

1. Preheat the oven to 350°F.

2. Heat the oil in a sauté pan over medium heat, add the onion, and sauté for 3 minutes, or until softened.

3. Add the bell pepper and sauté for another 2 minutes, then add the salt, cumin, and garlic and sauté for 1 minute.

4. Remove the mixture from the pan and place in a bowl. After the mixture has cooled, add the chicken, corn, and 1 cup of the cheese and mix to combine.

5. Pour half the enchilada sauce into a 9 x 11-inch baking dish.

6. Divide the chicken mixture evenly among the tortillas, placing it in the middle of each tortilla and rolling it up like a wrap.

7. Place the rolled enchiladas close together, seam side down, in the sauced baking dish and pour the rest of the enchilada sauce on top. Sprinkle the enchiladas with the remaining ½ cup cheese.

8. Cover the dish with foil and bake for 15 minutes, then uncover and bake 5 minutes more, and serve.

TO FREEZE: *Cover the enchiladas with foil at the end of step 7 and freeze for up to 4 months. When ready to serve, place the covered frozen enchiladas in a preheated 350° oven and bake for 30 minutes, uncovering them in the last 5 minutes.*

ᴛᴠ rice-cooker mac and cheese

4 to 6 servings

2 cups uncooked pasta (macaroni, ziti, farfalle, bugles—your choice!)

1½ cups low-sodium chicken broth

1 teaspoon kosher salt

1 cup whole milk

1½ cups three-cheese blend (such as Cheddar, mozzarella, and Monterey Jack)

Add-ins: chopped broccoli, cauliflower, carrots or butternut squash, or frozen peas

I don't know many kids who don't like macaroni and cheese. I love making my own, but even for someone like me who wants everything to be homemade, it's not always easy. Between cooking the pasta, making the sauce, and then baking it, the process can take time that we moms just don't have. But as time-consuming as the homemade kind can be, I just can't break down and buy the powdered cheese version in the box, no matter how simple it may be to prepare.

If you have a rice cooker (and I hope you do, because it is one of the great time-saving pieces of equipment), this recipe is going to change your family's world! All you have to do is put all of the ingredients into the rice cooker and let it do the rest of the work for you. The best part is that you can tailor this recipe to your child's favorite tastes and flavors. For example, if you want to give it some added nutrition, just throw in a few veggies. This recipe is also a great way to involve your kids in cooking, as they can be in charge of placing the ingredients in the cooker.

Now, what are you going to do with all that time you just saved being a kitchen hero to your kids?

JEN: I bought a rice cooker just to make your Rice-Cooker Mac and Cheese! Every time I make it, my daughter insists on jumping on our trampoline while it cooks—just like you and Kenya do in the video!

1. Place the pasta, stock, and salt in the rice cooker, cover, and cook for 15 minutes.

2. Open the lid, add the milk, cheese, and any desired add-ins, stir to combine, close the lid, and cook for 20 minutes. You can add an additional 5 minutes if you prefer a golden crust on the bottom. Serve.

NOTE: *Rice cookers can cook at different temperatures, so make sure to check your mac and cheese once or twice after it cooks for 30 minutes.*

un-fried chicken tenders

Growing up in Kentucky, a huge bucket of the Colonel's original recipe was a staple at parties and family gatherings. I can still remember peering over the edge of the container with my grease-covered fingers and seeing even more grease pooled at the bottom of the oversize tub of chicken. I guess that's what made it "finger lickin' good," but since I try to avoid fast food altogether now, I prefer my version of un-fried chicken. It's super-crunchy on the outside and tender inside, but *a lot* more healthy.

1. Preheat the oven to 375°F and coat a baking sheet with cooking spray.

2. Whisk the bread crumbs, salt, paprika, garlic powder, and flour in a shallow bowl.

3. In a separate bowl, whisk the eggs with 2 tablespoons water.

4. Coat the chicken tenders in the egg mixture and then transfer them to the bread-crumb mixture. Press down with the heel of your hand to adhere the bread crumbs to the tenders.

5. Place the tenders on the baking sheet and lightly and evenly coat the tops of each tender with cooking spray.

6. Bake the tenders for 5 minutes and remove them from the oven. Turn the tenders over, spray them lightly and evenly again with cooking spray, and bake for 5 minutes more, or until cooked through, then serve.

TIP: *This recipe can also be made with pounded boneless, skinless chicken breasts.*

4 servings

Olive or canola oil cooking spray

1 cup Italian bread crumbs

¼ teaspoon kosher salt

¼ teaspoon paprika

¼ teaspoon garlic powder

2 tablespoons all-purpose flour

2 large eggs

1 pound chicken tenders

brown rice and veggie casserole

4 to 6 servings

1 small onion

2 celery stalks, roughly chopped

1 medium carrot, roughly chopped

1 cup cauliflower florets

1 cup broccoli florets

1 tablespoon olive oil

⅓ cup plus ½ cup weelicious Tomato Sauce (page 116), or your favorite pasta sauce

⅓ cup plus ½ cup ricotta cheese

One 8-ounce package mozzarella cheese, shredded (about 1½ cups)

2 cups cooked short-grain brown rice

½ teaspoon kosher salt

Just when did casseroles go out of culinary fashion? I think they were just the victim of being the punchline once too often in 1970s sitcoms. When I was a kid my mother made casseroles all the time. For my eighteenth birthday party, I asked her to make one of her casseroles that I still dream about today. Moms don't seem to make casseroles the way they used to, but they should. Done the right way, they can make an awesome family dinner.

Trying to get a protein, carbohydrate, and veggie into every meal isn't always possible, but casseroles make it a lot easier to try. I like to make this Brown Rice and Veggie Casserole and keep it in the fridge for a few days, so whenever someone's hungry I've got a meal ready to go. With gooey cheese and tiny bits of veggies throughout, it's a recipe that even the smallest of eaters can enjoy.

I'm bringing the casserole back!

1. Preheat the oven to 375°F and grease an 8 x 8-inch baking dish.

2. Place the onion, celery, carrot, cauliflower, and broccoli in a food processor and pulse to chop into bite-size pieces (you can also do this by hand).

3. Heat the oil in a large sauté pan, add the vegetables, and sauté for 6 minutes, or until fork-tender.

4. Transfer the cooked vegetables to a large bowl, add ⅓ cup of the pasta sauce, ⅓ cup of the ricotta, and 1 cup of the mozzarella, and stir to combine.

5. In a separate bowl, combine the brown rice, salt, and the remaining ½ cup pasta sauce, ½ cup ricotta, and ½ cup mozzarella.

6. Press half of the rice mixture (about 1½ cups) into the baking dish. Spread all of the vegetable mixture on top, followed by the remaining brown rice mixture.

7. Bake for 50 minutes, remove from the oven, and allow to rest at room temperature for 30 minutes.

8. Cut into squares and serve.

TIP: *You can freeze the casserole for up to 4 months before or after baking.*

turkey pesto meatballs

4 to 6 servings

1¼ pounds ground turkey

¼ cup pesto (homemade—see pages 107–108 or weelicious.com for options—or your favorite brand)

¼ cup bread crumbs

¼ cup grated Parmesan cheese

1 teaspoon salt

2 cups weelicious Tomato Sauce (page 116) or other pasta sauce

A weelicious reader e-mailed me once to say that she had tried a version of these meatballs at a friend's house, and while she knew the flavors and ingredients, she could not recall the recipe. I love getting requests from readers to figure out how to make dishes they love, because part of the fun of testing recipes for me is discovering potential new family favorites. I'm so grateful to that reader, because everyone under my roof *loved* these bite-size gems. Shockingly, fourteen-month-old Chloe downed the most—six in one meal! She probably would have eaten the whole batch had I let her, but even babies need to share!

1. Preheat the oven to 350°F.

2. Place the turkey, pesto, bread crumbs, cheese, and salt in a large bowl and use clean hands to combine them thoroughly.

3. Using about 1 tablespoon per meatball, roll the mixture into balls and set them aside on a plate.

4. Pour the tomato sauce into a 9 x 9-inch baking pan and lay the meatballs evenly over the sauce.

5. Cover the baking pan with foil and bake for 20 to 25 minutes, until cooked through.

6. Serve with pasta or rice and a nice salad.

TO FREEZE: *At the end of step 3, place the meatballs on a cookie sheet and freeze for 30 minutes. Place them in a zip-top bag, label, and freeze for up to 3 months. Before using, defrost them in the refrigerator for 24 hours and start at step 4, or put them straight into the oven with the sauce and increase the cooking time by 5 minutes.*

baked shells

6 servings

One 16-ounce box large pasta shells

1 tablespoon olive oil

1 small onion, diced

1 garlic clove, minced

1 pound ground turkey

1 teaspoon kosher salt

1½ teaspoons dried Italian herbs

1½ cups weelicious Tomato Sauce (page 116), or your favorite pasta sauce

1¼ cups ricotta cheese

½ cup grated Parmesan cheese

1 large egg

1 cup shredded mozzarella cheese

When I was growing up my mother would have evening charity meetings or dinners every week. My father had little to no cooking ability, so my mom kept a surplus of food stocked in the freezer. All Mom had to do on those nights she wasn't going to be home was take something out of the freezer and pop it in the oven, and we'd have a homemade meal just in time for her to run out the door.

These baked shells are always a hit with my family and remind me of the food my mother prepared when I was a kid. I usually double the recipe so we can have one batch for dinner that night and an extra one stored away in the freezer for the times I'm too tired to cook. Be happy if you have leftovers—you can always save a shell or two for your kid's lunch the next day!

1. Cook the shells according to package directions, taking care to keep them whole. Drain and set aside.

2. Preheat the oven to 375°F.

3. Heat the oil in a sauté pan over medium heat. Add the onion and sauté for 4 minutes, or until softened. Add the garlic and cook for 1 minute.

4. Add the turkey, salt, and Italian herbs. Cook the turkey, breaking it up as you cook, for 6 to 8 minutes, or until it is cooked through. Set the turkey mixture aside to cool.

5. Meanwhile, spread ½ cup of the tomato sauce in a 9 x 11-inch baking pan.

6. Place the cooled turkey mixture in a large bowl with the ricotta, Parmesan, and egg. Stir to combine.

7. Place 2 tablespoons of the turkey-cheese mixture in each pasta shell.

8. Nestle the shells in the sauce in the pan, seam side down.

9. Cover the shells with the remaining 1 cup tomato sauce and sprinkle the mozzarella on top.

10. Cover the pan with foil and bake for 30 minutes. Remove the foil and bake 10 minutes more, or until the cheese is melted and bubbly.

11. Serve with a salad or veggies if desired.

TO FREEZE: *Cover the baked shells with foil at the end of step 9 and freeze for up to 4 months. When ready to serve, place the covered shells in a pre-heated 375° oven and bake, covered, for 20 minutes, then uncover and bake for 10 more minutes.*

chicken teriyak-wee

4 servings

One 8-ounce can crushed pineapple, or 1 cup finely chopped fresh pineapple

½ cup low-sodium soy sauce

3 tablespoons honey or agave nectar

1 teaspoon grated fresh ginger

1 small garlic clove, minced

4 boneless, skinless chicken breasts (about 2 pounds)

1 teaspoon cornstarch

Parents often ask me for healthier versions of their favorite recipes, and hands down, one of the most requested is chicken teriyaki.

One of the biggest pitfalls of buying premade teriyaki sauce from the grocery is that most brands generally contain loads of corn syrup (a big no-no in my book!). I decided to play around with the dominant flavors in teriyaki sauce (pineapple, soy, and ginger) to see if I could produce my own healthy version that still retained teriyaki's great taste. I was thrilled with the results, and I'm not sure if I've ever received as many "this is incredible!" responses from my informal, online tasting group as I did with this dish.

For all of you out there who suggested it, thank you, and keep the ideas coming!

1. Place the crushed pineapple, soy sauce, honey, ginger, and garlic in a large bowl and whisk to combine.

2. Place the chicken breasts in a bowl, cover them with two thirds of the teriyaki sauce (reserve the remaining sauce), and refrigerate for 30 to 60 minutes, or overnight.

3. Preheat the broiler and place the rack in the middle position.

4. Place the marinated chicken breasts on a foil-lined baking sheet and broil for 8 to 10 minutes on each side, for a total of 16 to 20 minutes. Discard the marinade.

5. While the chicken is broiling, place the reserved teriyaki sauce in a saucepan, add the cornstarch, and whisk continuously over medium heat for 1 minute, or until thickened.

6. Slice the chicken, pour the sauce on top, and serve.

TIP: *Keeping the chicken in the marinade overnight will make it even tastier.*

TIP: *Instead of broiling, the chicken can also be grilled for 6 minutes on each side.*

lasagna rolls

Growing up, I loved my mom's lasagna, and now that I'm a mother, I love making it for my own family. It's a hearty and healthy dish that turns any meal into a special occasion.

I thought it would be fun to send Kenya to school with some lasagna for his lunch but knew it would be too messy for a three-year-old. I played around a bit, and the result was these lasagna rolls. They're really great for kids because kids love little individualized portions. They're also easy on Mom and Dad because they fit snugly in your little one's lunch box without making a mess. The best part about this dish? It's got a carbohydrate, vegetable, protein, and dairy, so you can be assured your family is eating a balanced meal all in one dish!

1. Preheat the oven to 375°F. Cook the lasagna noodles according to package directions. Drain and set aside.

2. In a large bowl, whisk the egg, ricotta, ¼ cup of the Parmesan, the Italian herbs, salt, ½ cup of the mozzarella, and the spinach until combined.

3. Place ¼ cup of the sauce on the bottom of a 9 x 11-inch baking dish.

4. Spread ⅓ cup of the ricotta mixture on each lasagna noodle, covering it fully, and roll it into a pinwheel.

5. Place the lasagna rolls seam side down in the baking dish and top with the remaining sauce, ½ cup mozzarella cheese, and ¼ cup Parmesan.

6. Cover the dish with foil and bake for 30 minutes.

7. Uncover, continue to bake for an additional 15 minutes, and serve.

TO FREEZE: *Prepare the dish through step 6, cover, and freeze for up to 4 months. When ready to eat, bake for 45 minutes covered and 15 minutes uncovered.*

9 lasagna rolls, 4 to 6 servings

9 lasagna noodles, cooked (I recommend cooking a few extra noodles in case one breaks)

1 large egg

One 16-ounce container ricotta cheese

½ cup grated Parmesan cheese

1 teaspoon dried Italian herbs

1 teaspoon kosher salt

1 cup shredded mozzarella cheese

1 cup cooked, finely chopped spinach or broccoli (frozen vegetables that are drained well work great in this recipe)

1½ cups weelicious Tomato Sauce (page 116) or your favorite brand

slow-cooker bbq chicken

4 to 6 servings

4 skinless, bone-in chicken breasts

1 cup barbecue sauce (see Note)

I came up with this recipe one summer when most of the country was in the midst of an oppressive heatwave. It was so hot here in California that the mere thought of turning on my oven or grill held absolutely no appeal. That was a drag, because it wouldn't be summertime for our family without barbecued chicken. Thank goodness for one of my favorite pieces of kitchen gear: the slow cooker!

All you do is place the chicken and sauce in the slow cooker, coat it well, cover, walk away, and within 2½ hours you'll have chicken that's so juicy and tender you won't believe it takes so little effort.

With the kids out of school and tons of summer activities to enjoy, wouldn't you rather be spending the scant free time you have with your little ones rather than working in the kitchen? Plus, no matter how hot it is outside, when you put this Slow-Cooker BBQ Chicken on the table, everyone inside will think you're cool.

AUTUMN: **This is so yummy. Had it for dinner this evening and my house smelled wonderful. It's much better than putting the chicken in the oven—my house is cooler and the chicken is so tender that it just falls apart! I ended up cooking it on high for about 2 hours. Definitely going to do this one again soon!**

1. Place the chicken in a slow cooker.

2. Pour the barbecue sauce over the chicken and coat the chicken well with the sauce.

3. Cook the chicken on low for 2½ hours and serve. Save the juice from the bottom of the pot if you want to make Shredded BBQ Chicken Sammies (page 171).

NOTE: *I toyed around with making my own barbecue sauce for this recipe, but there are so many great sauces on the market now made without corn syrup, I use a good bottled brand.*

shredded bbq chicken sammies

Pulled pork sandwiches are a popular summer recipe, but these Shredded BBQ Chicken Sammies are a lot healthier and *so* easy to make. I eat barbecue sauce on everything from shrimp to chicken to baked potatoes, so it's no surprise to me that my kids love BBQ, too.

I love whipping up Slow-Cooker BBQ Chicken for Sunday night dinner because of all of the great things you can do with the leftovers. I like to shred them for sammies for school lunch on Monday and for quesadillas on Tuesday. That covers *three* meals, from just one easy-to-prepare recipe.

1. Using two forks or your hands, pull the chicken into bite-size pieces.

2. Combine the shredded chicken with the liquid from the slow cooker.

3. Place one quarter of the mixture on a bun or roll and cover with additional barbecue sauce. Repeat with the remaining chicken and buns and serve.

4 servings

2 chicken breasts from Slow-Cooker BBQ Chicken (page 170)

½ cup liquid from the slow cooker

ACCOMPANIMENTS

Barbecue sauce and rolls or sandwich buns

vegetable frittata

4 servings

8 large eggs

½ teaspoon kosher salt

1 tablespoon vegetable or canola oil

3 cups chopped vegetables, such as mushrooms, spinach, broccoli, cauliflower, kale, chard, zucchini, or bell peppers

1 cup cherry tomatoes, halved

¾ cup shredded Cheddar or mozzarella cheese

ACCOMPANIMENT

a side of bacon or ham

One time our usual Sunday farmers' market trip coincided with both the Los Angeles Marathon *and* a downpour, so most of the roads were blocked off and the ones that weren't were backed up with traffic. Since none of us were in the mood to brave the rain or gridlock, we opted to stay in for a lazy Sunday at home. This meant that we were without our usual post-market kitchen bounty, and so we relied on whatever was in the fridge for dinner.

There were some eggs left over from the previous Sunday's outing and a random assortment of veggies, so I decided to make us a frittata. While I was busy prepping the ingredients, Kenya decided the frittata needed dinosaur kale from our garden, and so on went his and Chloe's rain gear so they could go out and harvest it.

Even though the ingredients required to make a frittata are identical to what you would use in a simple omelet, for me, taking those same ingredients and making a frittata is a thing of magic. When I pulled this beautiful creation out of the oven and slid it onto a cutting board to slice up for my impressed family, I thought to myself, *If this is what I can make when I'm just relying on what's lying around the fridge, I'm looking forward to a lot more rainy Sundays at home.*

1. Preheat the oven to 350°F.

2. Whisk the eggs and salt in a bowl and set aside.

3. Heat the oil in a medium ovenproof sauté pan over medium heat, add the vegetables, and sauté for 5 minutes, or until tender.

4. Pour the eggs over the vegetables and top evenly with the cherry tomatoes and shredded cheese.

5. Bake for 25 minutes, or until cooked through.

6. Slice into wedges and serve with bacon or ham.

chicken parmesan wheels

4 servings

4 boneless, skinless chicken breasts (about 2 pounds total)

½ teaspoon kosher salt

1 cup baby spinach leaves

1 cup shredded mozzarella cheese

¼ cup grated Parmesan cheese

2 large eggs

½ cup bread crumbs

¼ cup all-purpose flour

1 tablespoon vegetable or canola oil

Whenever my mother had a dinner party, she would always let me be her little helper. I took great pride in being around the adults and part of the parties, but I took even greater joy in sampling the special dishes she made, such as chicken stuffed with cheese and ham. I wanted to make a similar version of that dish for this book but decided to try something a bit healthier, stuffing mine with spinach. I also use mozzarella and Parmesan cheeses, similar to a traditional Italian chicken parm. My last variation was serving these in the shape of wheels, which added a ton of appeal for the kids. With all these changes, this may not ultimately resemble my mom's dish, but at least she was responsible for the inspiration!

1. Preheat the oven to 350°F.

2. Place the chicken between two pieces of plastic wrap and use a meat mallet to pound them to ¼ inch thick. Season the chicken with the salt.

3. Top each piece of chicken with the spinach, mozzarella, and Parmesan, roll the breasts into cylinders, and secure them with toothpicks.

4. Whisk the eggs in a medium bowl and mix in 1 tablespoon water. In a separate bowl, combine the bread crumbs and flour.

5. Roll each breast in the egg, then coat it in the bread crumb mixture.

6. Heat the oil in a large ovenproof skillet over medium-high heat and sear the chicken rolls on all sides for a total of 2 minutes.

7. Transfer the skillet to the oven and bake for 16 to 18 minutes, until cooked through. Set aside to rest for 5 minutes.

8. Slice the breasts into 1½-inch-thick wheels and serve.

shrimp tacos

We love our local Mexican restaurant so much that my husband and I even had our wedding party there. Every now and then we take the kids there for dinner and always order the same thing: shrimp tacos. They come out unadorned, and my guys love the interactive aspect of rolling them up and dipping them in a side of "no spicy" guacamole, as they call it.

It's fun to go out to eat as a family, but it can be expensive, and tacos are so easy to make that you really don't need a restaurant. In fact, whenever we play "restaurant" at home (a game that always gets my kids to eat come dinnertime), this and a side of Big Kid Guacamole is frequently on the menu.

1. Heat the oil in a large sauté pan over medium heat. Add the onion and sauté for 3 minutes, or until softened.

2. Add the shrimp, salt, cumin, and lime juice and sauté for 3 to 4 minutes, until the shrimp are cooked through.

3. Top with the cilantro and stir to combine.

4. Serve with warm corn tortillas and the suggested accompaniments.

4 servings

1 tablespoon vegetable or canola oil

1 small onion, diced

1 pound uncooked large shrimp, peeled and deveined

½ teaspoon salt

½ teaspoon ground cumin

1 tablespoon lime juice

2 tablespoons chopped fresh cilantro

8 corn tortillas, warmed through

ACCOMPANIMENTS

Big Kid Guacamole (page 110), sour cream, rice, grated cheese, salsa, chopped romaine lettuce

cheesy chicken taquitos

**12 taquitos,
serves 4**

1 pound boneless,
skinless chicken breasts

¼ teaspoon garlic
powder

½ teaspoon kosher salt

1 teaspoon ground
cumin

1 cup shredded
Mexican cheese blend
or Cheddar cheese

12 corn tortillas

Olive or canola oil
cooking spray

Avocado Lime Sauce
(page 111), for serving

I love taquitos, but most of the time when you find them, either at a fast-food chain or your local Mexican restaurant, they're deep-fried to make them extra-crisp. They're delicious, but I was intent on making an equally appealing, yet healthier version.

I serve these with a kid-friendly avocado sauce for dipping, which my friends love as much as their kids do. Maybe I should call this incredibly easy-to-prepare dish *everyone-friendly*.

1. Preheat the oven to 400°F.

2. Place the chicken in a steamer pot over boiling water and steam for 10 to 15 minutes, until cooked through. Set aside to cool slightly.

3. Use a fork to shred the chicken into small pieces. Set aside to cool.

4. Combine the chicken in a bowl with the garlic powder, salt, cumin, and cheese.

5. Place 2 corn tortillas at a time in between two damp paper towels and microwave for 20 to 30 seconds to soften them (this will also prevent them from cracking when rolling).

6. With 1 tortilla in front of you, place 2 tablespoons of the chicken mixture on the side closest to you and roll it up. Repeat with the rest of the tortillas and filling.

7. Place the taquitos seam side down on a foil-lined baking sheet, spray the tops lightly with cooking spray, and bake for 25 minutes, or until crisp.

8. Serve with Avocado Lime Sauce.

TO FREEZE: *After step 6, the taquitos can be frozen in labeled zip-top bags for up to 3 months. When ready to eat, continue from step 7.*

TIP: *If you have leftover rotisserie chicken, use 2 cups and follow from step 4.*

mac, chicken, and cheese bites

20 mini bites

Olive or canola oil cooking spray

2 tablespoons unsalted butter

2 tablespoons all-purpose flour

½ teaspoon kosher salt

1½ cups milk

1 cup shredded Cheddar cheese

½ cup grated Parmesan cheese

1 cup cooked diced chicken

½ pound cooked elbow macaroni

¼ cup bread crumbs

At the moment, both of my kids are going through a serious macaroni and cheese phase. It's funny how kids get something in their heads and just fixate on it. This has happened to Kenya with lots of foods, such as pizza, pasta, yogurt, muffins, cheese, and even string beans. Now he and Chloe are obsessed with mac and cheese.

These Mac, Chicken, and Cheese Bites are a tasty way to give your kids a double boost of protein. I especially love them because they fit beautifully in a lunch box, and even little kids who can't yet use utensils can easily hold them in their hands. When Kenya first saw these and asked what they were, I answered, "Mac and cheese muffins." They were a winner before he even tried the first bite! I wonder if that means this phase will last three times as long?

1. Preheat the oven to 400°F.

2. Spray a mini muffin pan or regular 8-cup muffin pan with cooking spray.

3. In a small saucepan over medium heat, melt the butter, whisk in the flour and salt, and cook for 2 minutes, whisking constantly until thick.

TAMMY: I love making the Mac, Chicken, and Cheese Bites. They're easy and freeze well. My almost two-year-old has recently become a picky eater, but I can always count on him eating these! I've started to add pureed sweet potatoes to the cheese sauce and/or some small veggies, like cut-up carrots and peas, to up the veggie factor. Even the ladies at day care have commented on how yummy they smell and look!

4. Add the milk in a slow stream, whisking to combine. Bring the mixture to a boil, whisking constantly, then reduce to a simmer. Cook for about 3 minutes, stirring constantly, until thickened.

5. Add the Cheddar cheese and ¼ cup of the Parmesan cheese. Stir until melted.

6. In a large bowl, combine the cheese sauce, chicken, and cooked pasta and stir to combine.

7. In a small bowl, combine the remaining ¼ cup Parmesan cheese and the bread crumbs.

8. Place 1 tablespoon of the macaroni mixture into each mini muffin cup or ¼ cup if using regular muffin cups. Sprinkle the tops with the bread and cheese mixture.

9. Bake for 18 to 20 minutes, until golden brown, or 25 minutes for regular-size muffins.

10. Cool in the muffin cups, remove, and serve.

TO FREEZE: *Cool the bites thoroughly, place them in a zip-top bag, label, and freeze for up to 4 months. When ready to eat, place the bites in a toaster oven or 300°F oven for 10 minutes, or until heated through.*

veg-wee burgers

**4 burgers or
8 mini burgers**

½ cup bulgur wheat

One 15-ounce can
pinto beans, rinsed and
drained

½ cup grated Monterey
Jack cheese

½ cup grated carrot

½ teaspoon salt

½ teaspoon garlic
powder

½ teaspoon onion
powder

1 tablespoon canola or
vegetable oil

ACCOMPANIMENTS

Bread, pitas, or
hamburger buns,
lettuce, tomato,
ketchup, mustard,
mayonnaise, avocado,
pickles

Compared to so many other prepared foods you can buy at the grocery, frozen veggie burgers do seem really healthy (and some brands are certainly better than others). The problem is that many of them are packed with sodium, additives, and fillers. They also can be pretty expensive, with the "healthier" brands coming out at well over a dollar per burger.

This veggie burger recipe is nutritious, really easy to make, and freezes beautifully, so you get all the convenience and great taste of store-bought brands, only healthier and much cheaper. On those nights when you're in a hurry, you'll be glad to know you have a few of these in the freezer all ready to heat up, pop in buns, and chow down with your gang!

1. Place the bulgur wheat and 1 cup water in a small pot. Bring to a boil, then reduce the heat, cover, and simmer for 15 minutes, or until the water is absorbed. The bulgur will be slightly al dente. Set aside to cool.

2. Place the pinto beans in a food processor and puree.

3. In a large bowl, combine the beans, cheese, carrot, salt, garlic and onion powders, and cooked bulgur and mix thoroughly.

4. Evenly divide the mixture and form it into patties.

5. Heat the oil in a large sauté pan over medium heat and cook the burgers for 3 minutes on each side.

6. Serve with your desired accompaniments.

LISA: **The Veg-Wee Burgers were a big favorite at my house just after my twins started eating a lot of solids because they're packed with great stuff they might not have eaten individually. But when mixed together and sautéed in a skillet to add a little crispiness, they were devoured immediately.**

TO FREEZE: *The patties can be frozen on a baking sheet for 1 hour and placed in a large zip-top bag or individually wrapped and frozen for up to 4 months. When ready to eat, defrost and then cook.*

bbq chicken quesadilla

I realized something interesting about my kids: I can put almost anything in a quesadilla and they will eat it. Two warm tortillas sandwiching melted cheese and whatever fillings they love—it's the perfect hand-held wedge-cut food that they can eat for dinner, in their school lunch, or even as a last-minute snack.

We make Slow-Cooker BBQ Chicken so often that it seems like we've got leftovers of it in the fridge at all times. Never wanting to waste a morsel of food, I'll go to great lengths to reinvent dinners using what we ate the night before in order to make something that my family doesn't notice as boring old leftovers. Quesadillas are a foolproof way to do that.

1. Place 1 tortilla in a dry pan over medium heat.

2. Spread 1 tablespoon of the BBQ sauce over the tortilla, sprinkle ½ cup of the cheese over the sauce, and ½ cup of the shredded chicken over the cheese.

3. Top with a second tortilla and heat through, about 3 minutes on each side, until the cheese is melted and the tortilla is slightly toasted.

4. Repeat for the second quesadilla.

5. Cut into wedges and serve.

2 to 4 servings

4 whole wheat, spelt, or white flour tortillas

2 tablespoons BBQ sauce

1 cup Monterey Jack or mozzarella cheese

1 cup shredded Slow-Cooker BBQ Chicken (page 170)

mexican lasagna

6 to 8 servings

Cooking oil spray

6 small corn tortillas, cut into quarters

1 large egg

¼ cup milk

¼ cup sour cream

1 cup mild chunky salsa

1 pound chicken breast, cooked and shredded

4 ounces cream cheese, cut into ½-inch cubes

2 tablespoons chopped fresh cilantro

3 scallions, chopped

1 teaspoon kosher salt

2 cups Mexican cheese blend (or a blend of Monterey Jack and mild Cheddar)

It's not always easy to come up with a reasonably priced recipe to feed a crowd, but this one is a no-brainer. Layered with rows of tortillas, chicken, cheese, and salsa, it's a great recipe for every age group. I especially like to make it for my and hubby's date night!

1. Preheat the oven to 350°F and spray a baking sheet with oil.

2. Place the quartered tortillas on the baking sheet and lightly spray the tops with oil.

3. Bake for 5 minutes and set aside.

4. In a large bowl, whisk the egg. Add the milk, sour cream, salsa, chicken, cream cheese, cilantro, scallions, and salt. Stir to combine.

5. Spray a 7 x 11-inch baking dish with oil. Arrange half of the quartered tortillas in the dish. Spread half the chicken mixture on top of the tortillas, then sprinkle 1 cup of the cheese blend on top.

6. Make a second layer with the rest of the tortillas, followed by the remaining chicken mixture and cheese.

7. Bake, uncovered, for 35 minutes, or until the casserole is bubbling and the cheese is nicely melted.

KIM: **We love the Mexican Lasagna! It's a hit for the whole family. I work full time, so I love one-pot meals. It's nutritious and filling and we all love it, especially our two-and-a-half-year-old son.**

corn dog bites on a stick

One of the biggest questions I get from moms is "What should I make for my child's birthday party?" I ask myself that same question twice a year.

There can be a good deal of stress that comes along with serving a group of people of all different ages, so you want to pick something that's reasonably easy to make a lot of but especially fun for the kids to eat. These corn dogs on a stick are equally appealing to kids and adults, and a totally memorable party treat that's sure to impress everyone.

1. Preheat the oven to 400°F.

2. Combine the flour, cornmeal, baking powder, sugar, and salt in a medium bowl.

3. In a separate bowl, whisk together the egg, milk, and oil.

4. Slowly add the dry ingredients to the wet and stir to combine.

5. Spray a mini muffin pan with cooking spray. Drop 1 tablespoon of the batter into each mini muffin cup, place 1 piece of hot dog in the center, and drop 1 teaspoon of batter over the hot dog.

6. Place a stick in the center of each corn dog bite, making sure the stick pierces the hot dog. (*You can also bake first and insert the sticks after the bites cool.*)

7. Bake for 10 to 12 minutes, until golden.

8. Serve with your desired accompaniments.

TIP: *If you don't have ice pop sticks on hand, you can make these without them and serve as Corn Dog Mini Muffins.*

16 to 18 mini dogs

⅔ cup all-purpose flour

⅓ cup cornmeal

1 tablespoon baking powder

1 tablespoon sugar

¼ teaspoon salt

1 large egg

½ cup milk

1 tablespoon vegetable or canola oil

Olive or canola oil cooking spray

3 or 4 hot dogs or veggie dogs (your favorites—I like Morningstar and Smart Dogs), sliced into ½-inch pieces

Wooden ice pop sticks

ACCOMPANIMENTS

Ketchup, mustard, barbecue sauce

shrimp "fried" rice

4 servings

2 tablespoons toasted sesame or vegetable oil

2 large eggs, whisked

1 red bell pepper, diced

1 teaspoon minced fresh ginger

1 small garlic clove, minced

1 pound uncooked shrimp, peeled and deveined (and cut into bite-size pieces if large; if using frozen shrimp, defrost and drain off all excess liquid)

2 cups cooked and cooled brown rice

2 scallions, sliced

½ cup frozen peas, defrosted

3 tablespoons low-sodium soy sauce

Toasted sesame seeds, for sprinkling

One of the hardest things about making dinner for your family is attempting to cook and watch your kids at the same time. Especially when you've got energetic little ones on your hands, multitasking in the kitchen can be tough. I learned this lesson well the day that Chloe took a Magic Marker and drew all over the kitchen counter and chairs while I was focused on getting her and Kenya's food on the table.

This fried rice recipe, which is a much healthier take on the Chinese restaurant classic, takes only a few minutes to cook. One of the keys to making it is having all your ingredients prepared beforehand. So that I can keep an eye on the kids and not wind up with unwanted artwork all over my furniture, I like to get the kids involved in the simple prep work. I set them both up at the counter next to me to chop ingredients (or pretend to chop, in Chloe's case), help peel the ginger with a spoon, and talk about what we're making. Not only do they get excited about eating their creation come dinnertime, but Mommy's sanity stays intact!

1. Heat 1 tablespoon of the oil in a wok or large sauté pan over medium heat. Add the eggs and scramble for 1 to 2 minutes, until cooked through. Remove the eggs to a small bowl and set aside.

2. Heat the remaining 1 tablespoon oil in the same skillet over medium-high heat, add the red bell pepper, ginger, and garlic, and stir-fry for 1 minute.

3. Add the shrimp and sauté for 2 minutes, stirring continuously. Add the cooked rice, scallions, and peas and cook for 1 minute more.

4. Add the scrambled eggs and soy sauce and cook for 1 minute, or until all the ingredients are thoroughly combined.

5. Sprinkle with sesame seeds (kids love to do this!) and serve.

orange chicken

If you were a child of the 1970s like me, your parents probably ordered a lot of Chinese takeout. I always begged mine to get Orange Chicken. It was sweet, simple, and of course yummy. These days I don't order out to enjoy Orange Chicken; I make it at home with this simple recipe. With a light citrus glaze and a few crunchy veggies thrown in for color and nutrition, this simple dish will be sure to take you back to those Sunday nights sitting at the dining room table, little white cartons opened everywhere, and the promise of a fortune cookie just a few bites away.

4 servings

1 cup orange juice

2 teaspoons peeled and grated fresh ginger

1 teaspoon honey

1 small garlic clove, minced

2 tablespoons low-sodium soy sauce

1 tablespoon vegetable or canola oil

1 pound boneless, skinless chicken breast, cubed

1 cup halved snow peas

1 red bell pepper, cut into 1-inch strips

Brown rice and orange wedges, for serving

1. Combine the orange juice, ginger, honey, garlic, and soy sauce in a small bowl.

2. Heat the oil in a large sauté pan over medium heat, add the chicken, and cook for 3 minutes, until browned on the outside and almost cooked through, stirring occasionally.

3. Add the snow peas and bell pepper and cook for 2 minutes, or until softened, then transfer the chicken-vegetable mixture to a bowl.

4. Add the orange juice mixture to the pan, bring to a boil, and cook for 5 minutes, or until reduced by half.

5. Add the chicken and vegetables back into the sauce and cook for 1 minute.

6. Serve with brown rice, with orange wedges on the side.

slow-cooker pulled pork tacos

6 to 8 servings

1 tablespoon ground cumin

1 teaspoon garlic powder

1 teaspoon chili powder

1 teaspoon onion powder

1 teaspoon paprika

1 teaspoon dried oregano

1 tablespoon kosher salt

One 3½- to 4-pound pork shoulder, rinsed and patted dry

One 16-ounce jar mild salsa

1 package small corn or flour tortillas

ACCOMPANIMENTS

Salsa, Big Kid Guacamole (page 110), chopped cilantro, diced onion, shredded cheese, sour cream

Grandparents are the best! Thank goodness for the days when I'm totally overwhelmed and they come to take Kenya on an outing. My dad has really surprised me with how much he loves playing with his grandson. They've gone together to see trains, the zoo, and even the golf course (I think I know who has more fun on that outing). What always accompanies these little jaunts is a meal or two. Quite often, when Kenya will come home holding a half-eaten imitation cheese sandwich on the whitest bread I've ever seen. Once he returned with a pulled pork taco. I looked at my dad as if he had two heads. "Really, Dad? You got a three-year-old a pulled pork taco?" Dad reassured me that Kenya had ordered it on his own—oh, yeah, blame the kid! To my amazement, though, Kenya sat down at our table and devoured it.

I became obsessed with re-creating the amazing pulled pork from our local taco stand. It's so soft, tender, and juicy that it must take hours to get that "fall off the bone" consistency. I've made my version repeatedly and it disappears so fast I can't keep the leftovers around long enough to savor them for myself. At least it's easy to make more, and because I use the slow cooker, there's next to no work for me.

Thank you to all the grandparents in our lives who are not only nurturing and caring for our precious little ones but hopefully turning them on to foods and adventures that we may not always think to do ourselves.

1. In a small bowl, combine the cumin, garlic powder, chili powder, onion powder, paprika, oregano, and salt.

2. Place the pork shoulder in the slow cooker and rub it all over with the seasoning mixture.

3. Pour the salsa around the pork shoulder.

4. Cook on low heat for 8 to 12 hours, until the meat comes apart easily when pulled with two forks.

5. Remove the pork to a plate and use the forks to shred it into bite-size pieces. Remove any visible fat.

6. Place the shredded pork in a serving dish along with some of the liquid from the pot and stir to combine.

7. Serve the shredded pork on tortillas with the desired accompaniments.

TIP: *To remove the excess fat from the juice around the pork, pour it into a cup and refrigerate until the fat solidifies on the top. The fat can then be easily scooped out, and only the juices will remain.*

MADELAINE: **I love this dish because it's so easy and so mouthwatering. It's perfect for a family meal. Thanks for making dinner prep so simple!**

MELANIE: **Thank you, thank you! Totally delicious and very easy for my little one to eat. I never would have thought to throw pork shoulder in a Crock-Pot like this. Weelicious hasn't let me down yet!**

KELLI: **I made this for supper tonight. It was wonderful, and all day my house smelled so good! It tasted just as good as it smelled, and was easy to prepare.**

JULIE: **I made these for adult margarita night and they were fabulous. The smell in the house was mouthwatering. They were a complete success, and everyone wanted the recipe. I had to laugh when I told them where I got the recipe. Thanks for including recipes the whole family can enjoy.**

SHARON: **This recipe is fabulous! I get rave reviews every time I make it.**

cold sesame soba noodles

4 to 6 servings

One 9.5-ounce package 100% buckwheat soba noodles

1 cup shelled frozen edamame, defrosted

1 small red bell pepper, cut into julienne strips

1 cup cubed firm tofu

¼ cup almond or peanut butter

2 tablespoons mayonnaise or Vegenaise

2 tablespoons Bragg Liquid Aminos or low-sodium soy sauce

1 tablespoon rice vinegar

2 teaspoons honey or agave nectar

1 small garlic clove

1-inch piece fresh ginger, peeled and chopped

1 tablespoon toasted sesame oil

¼ cup vegetable oil

Minced scallion and/or sesame seeds, for garnish

This is one of my favorite recipes, and it gets a great response from everyone, young and old alike. It's so easy to prepare that you probably already have most of the ingredients in your fridge already.

Soba noodles are made from buckwheat, a grain high in vitamin A, calcium, and selenium. You can also find a gluten-free variety (100% buckwheat), which makes them a great choice for kids with allergies or on gluten-free diets. Unlike pasta noodles, these cook in about 3 minutes, so don't walk away from the stove for too long!

This dish is perfect to take to a potluck meal or anytime you're feeding a crowd on a dime. I guarantee they'll love it.

1. Bring a large pot of water to a boil and add the soba noodles. Reduce the heat to a simmer and cook for 2 to 3 minutes, until just tender. Drain and run under cold water until the noodles are cool to the touch.

2. Add the noodles to a large bowl along with the edamame, bell pepper, and tofu.

3. To make the sauce, place the remaining ingredients in a blender or food processor and puree.

4. Pour the sauce over the noodles and toss to combine.

5. Serve with minced scallion and/or sesame seeds on top, if desired.

miso marinated fish

4 servings

½ cup yellow or white miso paste

2 tablespoons honey or agave nectar

½ cup mirin (rice wine)

1½ pounds black cod or salmon fillets (or other oily fish)

When I was living in New York City, I used to splurge with my girlfriends once in a while and dine at Nobu, a famed Japanese restaurant. Every dish on the menu is fantastic, but the miso cod is by far the crown jewel. It's been copied by many restaurants, but I have yet to taste one that comes close to matching the flavor and snap of the original. It's a unique recipe to be sure, but one you can make at home for a fraction of the restaurant price.

You can try different varieties of fish or even scallops, but black cod is always my first choice. It's high in omega-3 fatty acids and has a mild flavor that's perfect for kids.

There's no reason you can't enjoy the world's best dishes at home.

1. Combine the miso, honey, and mirin in a small bowl and whisk to combine.

2. Place the fish in a glass bowl or dish and pour the marinade on top. (Or to cut down on cleanup, you can marinate the fish in a zip-top bag.) Cover, refrigerate, and marinate from 30 minutes up to 24 hours, or even 2 days if you want deep, rich flavor.

3. When you're ready to cook, preheat the broiler to high.

4. Remove the fish from the marinade and place it on a foil-lined baking sheet.

5. Place the sheet in the broiler oven and broil for 8 to 10 minutes, until golden and bubbly.

6. Serve in Bibb lettuce cups or on top of brown rice, with steamed or sautéed baby bok choy, sugar snap peas, or any green veggie.

SHAWNNA: **It used to be that the only kind of fish they would eat was fish sticks. Then I made the Miso Marinated Fish and they loved it! It's a favorite of the whole family!**

baked ziti

I made this recipe for one of my dearest friends after she had her third baby. As busy and overwhelmed as she must have been with three kids in the house, she still made a point to e-mail me for the recipe. She said it was beyond scrumptious and made her whole family happy, so she wanted to re-create it for them ASAP.

I love making one-pot dishes like this one because you can do most of the work the day before and drop it off at a friend's house (or put it in your own oven) for a quick bake before dinner.

1. Preheat the oven to 350°F and spray a 9 x 11-inch baking dish with cooking spray.

2. In a large sauté pan over medium heat, heat the oil. Add the onion, bell pepper, and salt and sauté for 4 minutes. Add the garlic and cook 1 minute more.

3. Add the tomatoes and cook for 15 minutes. The sauce will thicken as it cooks.

4. Combine the sauce, pasta, and cheeses in a bowl and pour the mixture into the baking dish.

5. Bake uncovered for 30 minutes, or until bubbling and browned on top, and serve.

EMILY: **This was delicious and will be added to my favorite recipes for sure! Even my husband, who thinks every meal should include meat, ate it up.**

4 to 6 servings

Olive or canola oil cooking spray

1 tablespoon olive oil

½ onion, chopped (about ½ cup)

1 red bell pepper, finely chopped

1 teaspoon salt

1 garlic clove, minced

One 28-ounce can diced tomatoes

One 16-ounce box ziti pasta, cooked

2 cups grated mozzarella cheese

½ cup grated Parmesan cheese

chicken and wild rice casserole

4 servings

Olive or canola oil cooking spray

2 tablespoons olive oil

1 small onion, diced

1 cup sliced button mushrooms

1 teaspoon kosher salt

1 pound boneless, skinless chicken breasts, cut into ½-inch pieces

½ teaspoon garlic powder

½ cup sour cream

1 cup shredded Cheddar cheese, plus more for sprinkling on top

3 cups cooked wild rice

Do you ever crave dishes from your childhood? There has to be at least one recipe you wish you could make as well as your mom did (and maybe a bit more healthily). My mother made a great chicken and rice casserole, but I can still see the cream of mushroom soup plopping out of the can in the form of a gelatinous white cylinder. Although her recipe was yummy, I try to avoid cooking with anything that comes out of a can.

This is my version that's just as delicious as the one I ate as a kid, only more nutritious and a lot fresher!

1. Preheat the oven to 350°F and spray an 8 x 8-inch baking dish with cooking spray.

2. Heat 1 tablespoon of the olive oil in a large sauté pan over medium heat. Add the onion and sauté for 2 minutes, or until softened.

3. Add the mushrooms and ½ teaspoon of the salt and cook for 4 minutes, or until the mushrooms are tender and the onion is translucent. Set the vegetables aside in a bowl.

4. In the same pan, heat the remaining 1 tablespoon oil. Add the chicken, garlic powder, and remaining ½ teaspoon salt and sauté for 3 minutes, or until the chicken is lightly browned and cooked through.

5. In a large bowl, combine the vegetable mixture, chicken, sour cream, cheese, and wild rice. Spread the mixture in the baking dish and sprinkle with additional cheese.

6. Bake for 20 minutes, or until the cheese is melted and bubbly, and serve.

sweet broiled salmon

I think my kids could eat salmon every day of the week. They adore it plain, but I like to jazz it up a bit so they don't get bored! This is a perfect recipe for when you want to feed the kids but also impress any adults at the dinner table.

Salmon provides a good supply of omega-3 fatty acids and vitamin D and is a terrific source of protein. I buy wild salmon as often as possible, as there are so many documented concerns about the high levels of PCBs and antibiotics in farm-raised salmon. If you can't find it or it's too expensive, look for Pacific salmon, which is generally wild caught.

Served with simple steamed veggies and rice, this sweet entrée is easy to prepare and cleans up fast, so you'll impress everyone with a bare minimum of effort.

1. Place the honey, soy sauce, ginger, and vinegar in a bowl and whisk to combine.

2. Place the salmon fillets in a glass bowl and top with the marinade.

3. Marinate for 15 minutes on the counter (or up to 3 hours in the fridge).

4. Preheat the broiler.

5. Lay the fillets on a foil-lined sheet pan and place in the broiler. Broil for about 8 minutes, longer if the fillets are more than 1½ inches thick, taking care that they don't burn, until the salmon is just cooked through and the sauce is golden and bubbly.

6. Sprinkle the fish with toasted sesame seeds and serve.

TIP: *If you want to cut down on cleanup, you can pour the marinade into a zip-top bag with the fish and marinate.*

4 servings

2 tablespoons honey or agave nectar

2 tablespoons low-sodium soy sauce

2 teaspoons minced fresh ginger

1 tablespoon rice vinegar or cider vinegar

Four 4- to 6-ounce salmon fillets, skinned, rinsed, and patted dry

Toasted sesame seeds, for garnish (toast them briefly in a dry pan over low heat)

italian pasta pie

6 servings

10 large eggs

½ teaspoon kosher salt

2 tablespoons chopped basil leaves

½ cup shredded mozzarella cheese, plus more for sprinkling on top

2 tablespoons olive oil

1 small onion, diced

1 garlic clove, minced

¼ cup chopped sun-dried tomatoes

2 cups cooked rotini or fusilli pasta

1 cup cooked, shredded, and chopped chicken breast (about 1 chicken breast)

Almost every week I cook up big batches of pasta and chicken, so I know I've always got cooked food in the fridge ready to go for lunch and dinner. But even though you may have everything prepared ahead of time, it's still important to amp things up a bit so your troops don't suffer from mealtime monotony.

This is one of those beyond easy "dump, stir, and bake" meals that's almost impossible to mess up and makes enough to have for school lunch the next day. One less thing for Mommy to do!

1. Preheat the oven to 350°F.

2. In a large bowl, whisk the eggs, 2 tablespoons water, and the salt until fluffy. Add the basil and cheese, stir to combine, and set aside.

3. In a large oven-safe sauté pan, heat the oil over medium heat. Add the onion and sauté for 4 minutes, or until softened.

4. Add the garlic and sauté for 1 minute.

5. Stir in the sun-dried tomatoes, pasta, and chicken and stir until combined.

6. Pour the eggs over the pasta mixture and sprinkle additional cheese on top.

7. Cook for 2 minutes, or until the bottom is set (do not stir).

8. Place the pan in the oven and bake for 20 minutes, or until golden on top and cooked through.

9. Slice the pie into wedges and serve.

NOTE: *Be sure to prep all the ingredients for this recipe first. It's a great opportunity to use any vegetables you have on hand if you want to replace (or enhance) the sun-dried tomatoes or chicken.*

chicken and rice stir-fry

4 servings

2 tablespoons low-sodium soy sauce

1 tablespoon honey

1 tablespoon sesame, vegetable, or canola oil

½ pound ground chicken

1 small garlic clove, minced

1 teaspoon minced fresh ginger

1 cup grated carrots

¼ cup thinly sliced scallion

½ cup frozen peas, defrosted

2 cups cooked brown rice

2 teaspoons sesame seeds

Even if you can barely cook and have a profound fear of the kitchen, I promise that you can make a stir-fry. All you have to do is cut up some veggies and chicken, use some leftover brown rice from the Chinese takeout you probably ordered last night, heat a pan, and throw everything in. If you don't have all the veggies listed, improvise! You can add water chestnuts, broccoli florets, greens, or almost any other vegetables you've got sitting in the fridge. Make sure all your ingredients are cut up and ready to go and in less than six minutes you'll have a piping hot dinner ready to serve the whole family. See? Nothing to be scared of.

1. Combine the soy sauce and honey in a small bowl and set aside.

2. Heat the oil in a wok or large sauté pan over medium-high heat. Add the chicken, garlic, and ginger and sauté for 3 minutes, or until the chicken is cooked through, breaking it up as you saute.

3. Add the carrots, scallion, and peas and sauté for 2 minutes.

4. Add the cooked brown rice, soy sauce mixture, and sesame seeds and sauté for 1 minute, or until nicely blended and heated through, and serve.

bbq salmon

How many nights have you raced home with no idea how you were going to get fast, yet nutritious food on the table for your family? This is one of my 1-2-3 recipes for those desperate nights. Just swing by the supermarket on the way home, grab some salmon fillets and a bottle of good barbecue sauce, and you're good to go. If your family is anything like mine, they probably agree that barbecue sauce makes just about everything taste better. If you've never tried it on salmon, now's the time to give it a shot.

4 servings

½ cup your favorite barbecue sauce

2 tablespoons honey

1 pound salmon fillets, cut into 4 even pieces

1. Place the barbecue sauce and honey in a large bowl. Stir to combine.

2. Coat the salmon fillets in the BBQ sauce mixture, cover, and marinate for 20 to 30 minutes in the refrigerator.

3. Preheat the broiler. Line a baking sheet with foil.

4. Place the salmon fillets skin side down on the baking sheet and coat the top of the salmon fillets with the sauce from the bowl.

5. Broil for about 8 minutes, longer if the fillets are more than 1½ inches thick, taking care that they don't burn, and serve.

chicken satay burgers with peanut-coconut sauce

4 servings

1 pound ground chicken

⅓ cup chopped fresh cilantro

1 small garlic clove, minced

1 teaspoon minced fresh ginger

2 teaspoons low-sodium soy sauce

2 scallions, both white and green parts, chopped

1 tablespoon fresh lime juice

1 tablespoon canola or vegetable oil

Burger buns

Peanut-Coconut Sauce (recipe follows)

ACCOMPANIMENTS

Lettuce, cucumber slices, red onion slices

How many kids do you know who don't love burgers? I'd bet not many, but when you add some extra herbs and spices and serve with a creamy peanut-coconut dipping sauce on the side, it might be a race between the parents and the kids to see who devours these Chicken Satay Burgers first!

1. Place the chicken, cilantro, garlic, ginger, soy sauce, scallions, and lime juice in a bowl. Use your hands or a spatula to combine thoroughly.

2. Shape the mixture into 4 patties (or 8 patties for mini burgers). Moisten your hands to avoid sticking.

3. Heat the oil in a large sauté pan over medium-high heat and add the patties. Cook for 5 minutes (3 minutes for minis), flip, cover the pan, and cook for 4 minutes more (for either size).

4. Serve on buns topped with Peanut-Coconut Sauce and desired accompaniments.

peanut-coconut sauce

1. Place all the ingredients in a food processor and puree.

2. Serve with burgers, grilled fish, or chicken breasts.

Makes ½ cup

¼ cup peanut butter

2 tablespoon coconut milk

1 tablespoon low-sodium soy sauce

1 teaspoon toasted sesame oil

1 tablespoon rice vinegar

spaghetti pie

6 servings

Olive or canola oil cooking spray

2 large eggs, whisked

½ cup grated Parmesan cheese

8 ounces (½ package) spaghetti, cooked and tossed in a bowl with 1 teaspoon olive oil

1 tablespoon olive oil

1 pound ground turkey, beef, or chicken

½ teaspoon kosher salt

½ teaspoon garlic powder

½ teaspoon onion powder

One 16-ounce jar marinara sauce or weelicious Tomato Sauce (page 116)

1 cup ricotta cheese

½ teaspoon Italian herbs (or a combination of dried basil and oregano)

1 cup grated mozzarella cheese

If I make meals in the form of a muffin, cake, cookie, or pie, my kids are instantly intrigued. I've had great results with Sweet Beet Cookies (page 246), Breakfast Cupcakes (page 64), and Cottage Cheese Pancakes (page 66), but I really thought I hit the jackpot with Spaghetti Pie. When I told Kenya I was making him a Spaghetti Pie for dinner, he actually started giggling.

"What's Spaghetti Pie, Mommy?!"

"Well, it's . . . Spaghetti Pie!"

I realized that's all I had to say—he was sold.

1. Preheat the oven to 350°F degrees and coat a deep-dish pie pan with cooking spray.

2. In a small bowl, combine the eggs and ¼ cup of the Parmesan cheese. Add to the spaghetti and mix.

3. Transfer the spaghetti mixture into the pie plate and spread it to make a "pie crust."

4. Heat the oil in a large sauté pan over medium heat. Add the ground meat, salt, garlic powder, and onion powder and sauté for 5 minutes, or until the meat is cooked through.

5. Pour the marinara sauce over the meat and stir to combine.

6. In a bowl, combine the ricotta cheese, remaining ¼ cup Parmesan cheese, and Italian herbs.

7. Spread the ricotta-Parmesan mixture over the pasta, top with the marinara-meat mixture, and sprinkle on the mozzarella cheese.

8. Place the dish on a baking sheet and bake for 30 minutes, or until the cheese is melted and the pie is bubbling.

9. Allow the pie to rest for 10 minutes.

10. Cut into wedges and serve.

salmon noodle casserole

When I was a kid, tuna noodle casserole was big with our family. I love sharing my childhood favorite meals with my own kids, but like many of the casseroles from my early years, they were made with a lot of canned ingredients that, knowing what I do now, I don't want to serve my family.

In an effort to upgrade this dish a bit, I switched the tuna out for omega 3–packed salmon and use a simple cream sauce that only calls for a few basic ingredients. Now when I make this for dinner, it's like reliving my youth . . . only better.

1. Preheat the oven to 375°F and coat an 8 x 8-inch baking dish with cooking spray.

2. Melt the butter in a large saucepan over medium heat, add the onion, garlic, celery, and salt, and sauté for 4 minutes, or until the onion is softened.

3. Sprinkle in the flour and whisk until the vegetables are coated.

4. Slowly pour in the milk, whisking continuously for 3 or 4 minutes, until smooth and thickened.

5. Stir in the flaked salmon, pasta, and ½ cup of the cheese.

6. In a small bowl, combine the panko and the remaining ½ cup cheese.

7. Pour the salmon mixture into the baking dish and top with the panko-cheese mixture.

8. Bake for 25 minutes, or until the top is golden and bubbling, and serve.

4 to 6 servings

Olive or canola oil cooking spray

3 tablespoons unsalted butter

1 small onion, diced

1 small garlic clove, minced

½ cup diced celery

½ teaspoon salt

2 tablespoons all-purpose flour

1½ cups whole milk

Two 6-ounce cans boneless, skinless salmon, rinsed, or 1½ cups flaked cooked salmon

3 cups cooked pasta (such as fusilli, bowties, campanelle, or elbows)

1 cup grated Cheddar cheese

¼ cup panko or bread crumbs

mexican turkey meatloaf

4 servings

1½ pounds lean ground turkey

1 large egg

½ cup grated carrot

½ cup shredded Mexican cheese blend

¾ cup chunky mild salsa

½ teaspoon kosher salt

½ teaspoon garlic powder

½ teaspoon ground cumin

Most moms I know have a meatloaf recipe in their arsenal. But if you want to jazz yours up a bit, it's totally worth it to try this one. Even my hubby, who's not a big meat eater, had some for dinner and then made a sandwich with the leftovers the next day. And when Daddy's happy, everyone's happy.

1. Preheat the oven to 400°F and coat a 7 x 11-inch baking pan with cooking spray.

2. Place all the ingredients in a large bowl and stir or use your hands to combine thoroughly.

3. Shape the turkey mixture into a 3- to 4-inch-thick loaf in the baking pan.

4. Bake for about 45 minutes, uncovered, until a meat thermometer reads 160 to 165°F, and serve.

TIP: *If you want to serve these as individual Mexican Meatloaf Muffins, place in greased muffin cups and bake for 25 minutes at 400°F; 8 muffins.*

chicken bok choy lo mein

I find that if my husband and I enjoy a certain vegetable, our kids often follow suit. This is especially true when it comes to bok choy. It's one of my husband's favorite veggies, and so I tend to add it to a lot of my recipes at home. Now Kenya and Chloe love it, too. Mixed with noodles, chicken, a few other veggies, and a tangy sauce, this dish has a little something for everyone.

1. In a small bowl, combine the soy sauce, honey, and ginger. Put the chicken strips in a large bowl, add half the marinade, and set aside to marinate, reserving the remaining sauce.

2. Bring a large pot of salted water to a boil and cook the fettuccine according to package directions. Drain, rinse with cold water, and set aside.

3. Heat the oil in a wok or large sauté pan over high heat. Ad the onion and stir-fry for 2 minutes.

4. Add the chicken and stir-fry for 2 minutes more, or until cooked through.

5. Add the bell pepper and stir-fry for 1 minute, then add the boy choy and edamame and stir-fry 1 minute more.

6. Add the noodles and the reserved sauce and stir-fry for 1 minute, or until the noodles are heated through and coated.

7. Serve with the cashews, if using.

4 to 6 servings

¼ cup low-sodium soy sauce

1 tablespoon honey

1 teaspoon grated fresh ginger

1 pound boneless, skinless chicken breast, cut into thin strips

8 ounces (½ package) whole wheat fettuccine

2 tablespoons vegetable or canola oil

1 small onion, thinly sliced

1 red bell pepper, sliced

1 cup chopped baby bok choy

½ cup shelled edamame

¼ cup chopped cashews (optional)

sides

veggie nuggets

40 to 50 nuggets

2 large russet potatoes, peeled and cut into 2-inch cubes

2 medium carrots, peeled and cut into 1-inch pieces

1 cup broccoli florets

½ cup frozen corn kernels, defrosted

½ teaspoon kosher salt

½ teaspoon garlic powder

½ teaspoon onion powder

¼ cup all-purpose flour

2 large eggs, whisked

1 cup bread crumbs

Olive or canola oil cooking spray

Ketchup or mustard, for serving (optional)

I've received countless e-mails from moms asking if I have a recipe similar to the boxed veggie nuggets available at the grocery store. Finally, I broke down and bought some to see what all the fuss was about. Although labeled "all natural," the boxed nuggets contain tons of fillers that are totally unnatural in my eyes, so I decided to come up with my own version.

Not only are these nuggets out-of-this-world delicious, they're super-easy to make, and this recipe makes five times the number you get in a $5 box from the store. That's a $20 savings right there! Just pop what you don't use into labeled freezer bags and you're all set.

I have to say, if you're going to pick one super kid-friendly recipe to make from this book, you have to give this one a try!

1. Place the potatoes and carrots in a steamer pot over boiling water and steam for 15 minutes.

2. Add the broccoli and steam for 5 minutes.

3. Place the potatoes in a bowl and mash them. Place the corn, broccoli, and carrots in a food processor and pulse to finely chop.

4. Add the chopped vegetables, salt, garlic powder, and onion powder to the mashed potatoes and stir to incorporate.

5. Spread the mixture ½ inch thick on a baking sheet and freeze for 1 hour (no more than 1½ hours).

6. When you're ready to make the nuggets, place the flour, eggs, and bread crumbs in three separate bowls, forming an assembly line.

7. Preheat the broiler and line a baking sheet with foil. Coat the foil with cooking spray.

8. Remove the pan from the freezer. Use a 1- to 2-inch-wide cookie cutter to cut out shapes from the potato mixture, or use a knife to cut into small

squares. Gently coat the nuggets with the flour, then the egg, then the bread crumbs, and place on the baking sheet.

9. Lightly coat the nuggets with cooking spray. Broil for 2 minutes on each side, or until golden, keeping an eye on them so that they don't burn. (*You can also bake the nuggets at 450°F for 10 minutes.*)

10. Serve with ketchup or mustard if desired.

TO FREEZE: *After step 8, place the breaded nuggets on a baking sheet and freeze for 30 minutes. Remove from the freezer, place in a zip-top bag, label, and freeze for up to 3 months.*

italian corn kernels

4 to 6 servings

One 16-ounce package frozen corn kernels, defrosted

¼ cup Sun-Dried Tomato and Basil Pesto (page 107), or pesto of your choice

¼ cup grated Parmesan cheese

Occasionally when I'm trying to think of a vegetable side dish to serve the kids at dinner, I retreat to my comfort zone of steamed broccoli, edamame, or roasted potatoes. But on one of those nights when I was feeling a bit more inspired, I pulled out a few items I always keep on hand and came up with this simple, Italian-inspired corn dish. I should have given the kids shovels instead of forks, because they asked for thirds.

1. Place all the ingredients in a bowl and combine.

2. Serve cold, or heat for 2 minutes and serve warm.

potato pea cakes

If I had to guess two vegetables you probably have in your kitchen right now, I'd bet it's potatoes and frozen peas. Even when my cupboard is getting bare, it's rare that I don't have these two staples on hand. Just a bit of ketchup on the side for dipping makes these an irresistible side dish with tons of kid appeal.

1. Place the potato cubes in a steamer pot over boiling water and steam for 18 minutes, or until fork-tender.

2. Add the peas and steam for 2 minutes.

3. Set aside the potatoes and peas to cool.

4. Place the potatoes, peas, egg, flour, salt, onion powder, and garlic powder in a standing mixer and mix until combined (or combine in a large bowl).

5. Heat the oil in a large sauté pan over medium-high heat.

6. Shape the potato mixture into patties, using 2 tablespoons per patty and dusting them with flour if they're a bit sticky. Cook the patties for 2 minutes on each side, or until golden brown.

7. Serve with your desired accompaniments.

12 to 15 cakes

2 large potatoes (about 1 pound), peeled and cut into 2-inch cubes

1 cup frozen peas

1 large egg, whisked

¼ cup all-purpose flour

1 teaspoon salt

½ teaspoon onion powder

¼ teaspoon garlic powder

1 tablespoon vegetable or canola oil

ACCOMPANIMENTS

Ketchup, mustard, barbecue sauce

"fried" green beans with honey-mustard dipping sauce

4 servings

Olive or canola oil cooking spray

1 cup whole wheat panko or bread crumbs

½ teaspoon salt

½ teaspoon garlic powder

2 large eggs

¼ cup all-purpose flour

1 pound green beans

Honey-Mustard Dipping Sauce (recipe follows)

When I was a kid, one of my favorite activities was sitting next to my grandfather in front of huge bags of green beans that he had picked from the local U-pick farm and helping him snap off the ends. My grandfather loved to munch on the raw beans and chat the afternoon away with me. This year Kenya and Chloe planted their first bean stalk, and when the beans were finally ripe, the two of them had the best time picking them, snapping off the ends, and helping me steam them for dinner.

Fresh green beans need little beyond simple steaming, but after a summer full of simply prepared dishes I decided to test drive this version. My kids love almost any food with a crisp crust, and because these beans are actually baked, not fried, they're totally healthy. But the real star of this dish is the Honey-Mustard Dipping Sauce. Chloe loves dipping and dunking her veggies in it (and when she's run out of beans she has even tried to drink it!).

1. Preheat the oven to 450°F and coat a large baking sheet with cooking spray.

2. Combine the panko, salt, and garlic powder in a bowl, whisk the eggs in a second bowl, and place the flour in a third bowl.

3. Make an assembly line with the three bowls. Dip the green beans into the flour first, then the egg, and last into the panko mixture, coating the beans evenly. Repeat with all the beans.

4. Place the coated green beans on the baking sheet or on a baking rack on top of a baking sheet. Arrange the beans so that they're not touching, coat with more cooking spray, and bake for 30 minutes, or until the panko is golden.

5. Serve with the dipping sauce.

TO FREEZE: *After step 3, place the beans on a baking sheet and freeze for 30 minutes. Place the frozen beans in a zip-top bag, label the bag, and freeze up to 3 months. When you're ready to eat, take the beans out of the freezer and put them in the oven, adding at least another 3 to 5 minutes to the baking time.*

honey-mustard dipping sauce

Place the ingredients in a bowl, whisk until combined, and serve.

¼ cup yellow or Dijon mustard

1 tablespoon honey

spinach ricotta bites

20 bites

Olive or canola oil cooking spray

2 tablespoons unsalted butter

1 small yellow onion, chopped

1 garlic clove, minced

2 large eggs

1 cup low-fat or full-fat ricotta

½ cup shredded mozzarella cheese

½ cup grated Parmesan cheese

One 10-ounce package frozen chopped spinach, defrosted and very well drained (I use my hands to squeeze as much liquid out of the spinach as possible)

¼ teaspoon salt

Lucky for me that I have a cousin with two growing boys who loves to cook and feed her kids healthy food. She makes a version of this recipe in a pie dish and swears her boys absolutely devour it. Although sometimes I find statements like that hard to believe when we're talking about green foods and highly independent little boys, it makes me happy because I'm always game for recipes that defy the odds.

I decided to take my cousin's original recipe, make a few tweaks to the ingredients, and bake it in mini muffin cups instead of a pie dish, because it reduces the cooking time, and what kid doesn't like something mini? As for my initial doubts about this recipe's kid appeal, Kenya grabbed three of them from the cooling rack, and Chloe scarfed down four at dinner.

Flavorful, healthy, and *so* easy to make. My cousin Raleigh gets total props for this kiddie culinary hit!

1. Preheat the oven to 350°F and coat 20 mini muffin cups with cooking spray.

2. Melt the butter in a small sauté pan over medium heat. Add the onion and cook for 4 minutes, or until tender.

3. Add the garlic and sauté for 1 minute, then set aside to cool.

4. Whisk the eggs in a bowl. Stir in the ricotta, mozzarella, and Parmesan cheeses.

5. Stir in the spinach, salt, and the cooled onion and garlic mixture.

6. Pour the mixture evenly into the mini muffin cups.

7. Bake for 20 to 25 minutes, until the filling is set and golden on top, and serve.

 oven-baked "fries"

4 servings

3 russet potatoes, peeled and cut into fry shapes

2 tablespoons vegetable or canola oil

1 teaspoon kosher salt

ACCOMPANIMENTS

Ketchup, mustard, barbecue sauce

Not too long ago, I had the moment that many moms with kids older than mine have warned me about. I was in the car with Kenya when he looked out the window and said, "Mommy, what's that place over there with the playground and hamburgers on the sign?" Now, I grew up eating McDonald's, but now that I know what fast food is really made of, I'm committed to keeping my kids away from it for as long as possible. That doesn't mean that I want them to miss out on all of the fun foods I enjoyed as a kid (and still enjoy), like burgers and fries. I simply want them eating the healthiest possible versions of those foods, and through a lot of trial and error I've discovered that you can do so without sacrificing great flavor.

For example, take one of my favorites: french fries. Instead of deep-frying, I bake them in the oven. My "fries" come out crisp on the outside and tender on the inside, and I serve them up with a side of ketchup and mustard, just the way I used to like them when I was little.

Do you think if I take Kenya and Chloe to our neighborhood playground along with a sack of these it will be as pleasurable for them as McDonald's? My bet is as long as we're all together sharing fun and "fries," it will be!

1. Preheat the oven to 450°F.

2. Place the raw "fries" into a colander and rinse them under cold water to remove some of the starch. Pat them dry with a towel to remove as much moisture as possible.

3. Place the "fries" onto a baking sheet and toss them with the oil and salt to coat them evenly.

4. Bake for 20 minutes, then toss and bake for 10 minutes more, or until golden and starting to crisp.

5. Serve with your desired accompaniments.

rice and cheese treasures

How often does the clock strike 5:00 and you think, *Ugh, I haven't even thought about what to make for dinner!* On one of the many nights that happened to me, I came up with these Rice and Cheese Treasures, and they've since become a total favorite at our house. They're incredibly easy to prepare and they make a great lunch-box treat.

Whenever food appears fun or has a hidden surprise, kids tend to be excited about eating it. This dish satisfies both criteria: It's shaped like a ball (fun!) and has a cheesy center (surprise!). The first time I made them for Kenya, he took a bite, realized there was gooey, melted cheese inside his rice ball, and smiled from ear to ear. He looked up at me with utter joy and exclaimed, "Mommy, there's cheese!" Literally love at first bite.

**fourteen
1½-inch balls**

2 mozzarella or Cheddar cheese sticks

1 cup cooked brown or white rice (see Note)

2 tablespoons sesame seeds

1. Cut each cheese stick into 7 cubes (about ½-inch pieces).

2. Using moist hands to avoid sticking, place about 2 tablespoons of rice in the palm of your hand, then place a piece of cheese in the center and roll the rice into a ball around it. Repeat with the remaining rice and cheese pieces to make 14 rice balls.

3. Place the rice balls in a steamer pot over boiling water and cook for 2 minutes. If you don't have a steamer, place them on a plate in the microwave for 10 seconds, or just until the cheese melts.

4. Sprinkle the rice and cheese treasures with sesame seeds and serve.

NOTE: *It helps if the rice is sticky for this recipe, so if you're making it fresh, add a little more rice than the package directions call for. These work especially well with leftover Chinese takeout rice.*

spanakopita bites

30 bite-size triangles

One 10-ounce package chopped frozen spinach, defrosted and drained well (see Note)

½ cup crumbled feta cheese

1 cup ricotta cheese

1 large egg, whisked

½ teaspoon kosher salt

One 16-ounce package frozen phyllo dough, thawed

½ cup (1 stick) unsalted butter, melted

The inspiration for this Greek recipe came from my cousin in Kentucky. She always sends me suggestions for recipes based on foods her boys love, and believe it or not, spanakopita is one of them. It's a savory pastry comprised of flaky phyllo dough filled with spinach and feta cheese. The phyllo can be homemade, but it's a time-intensive process that is unnecessary because you can easily purchase high-quality prepared phyllo in the freezer section of your grocery. Spanakopita makes a fun lunch, snack, dinner, or even party hors d'oeuvre for your family because little kids can hold the individual servings in their hands.

I played around with this recipe a lot, worrying that it might be too involved compared with most of my recipes, but once you get the hang of making it, it doesn't take long at all. In my opinion, it's worth it. A bonus is that this recipe freezes beautifully, so you can store half of what you make now and just pop it into the oven on the nights you don't have time to cook.

Whether you're making this dish in Athens, Georgia, or Athens, Greece (or Louisville, Kentucky—thanks, cuz!), your family will definitely love you for it.

1. Preheat the oven to 375°F.

2. Place the spinach, feta, ricotta, egg, and salt in a bowl and mix thoroughly.

3. Place 1 sheet of phyllo on a clean, dry surface and use a pastry brush to brush it gently with melted butter. While you work, cover the remaining phyllo dough with a damp towel to prevent it from drying out.

4. Place another sheet of phyllo on top and brush it with more butter.

5. Add a third sheet of phyllo to the top of the stack, giving you a total of 3 layers. Do not brush the top layer with butter.

6. Cut the buttered stack into three 12 x 3-inch strips.

7. Place 1 tablespoon of filling on the closest corner of 1 strip, then fold the corner over to form a triangle. Continue folding over, like a flag, keeping a triangle shape. Repeat to make the rest of the triangles.

8. Place the triangles seam side down on a Silpat or parchment-lined baking sheet and lightly brush the tops with butter.

9. Bake the triangles for 20 minutes, or until golden brown, and serve.

NOTE: *To thoroughly remove the water from the spinach, drain it in a fine-mesh strainer and then squeeze it in a towel to remove any excess moisture.*

TO FREEZE: *After step 8, freeze the triangles on the baking sheet for 1 hour until solid, then place them in a zip-top bag, label, and freeze for up to 4 months. To bake them, continue from step 9. No need to defrost before baking.*

TIP: *To reheat leftover spanakopita, place them in a 400°F oven or toaster oven (not a microwave) for 5 minutes.*

mushroom barley

4 servings

2 tablespoons olive oil

1 small yellow onion, diced

¼ teaspoon sugar

1 cup chopped mushrooms

1 small garlic clove, minced

1 teaspoon kosher salt

3 cups low-sodium chicken broth

1 cup pearl barley, rinsed

Every holiday season, we go stay with my in-laws, who live in New York City. Although I do cook a few meals in their apartment, getting to order in most nights was like a serious mommy vacation for me. We called out for all kinds of different yummy food: Japanese, Chinese, Italian, and chopped salads and from an incredible local caterer. One night, my mother-in-law ordered some barley with mushrooms and onions and offered my daughter a taste. Chloe is a very good eater, but for whatever reason I didn't think she'd find this dish appealing at all. Enjoy it? She ate the entire pint.

I was so blown away that I ordered some more for the plane ride home. Chloe blew through all of that, too, before we were even halfway across the country. Never one to mess around when I find a healthy food that my whole family likes, I picked up the phone and called the caterer for his recipe. I'm not sure if I replicated his dish exactly, but the first time I made it for five kids that we had over for dinner, there were chimes of "all gone." Lucky for you this recipe is so easy that you'll never need to order out to enjoy it!

1. In a large pot, heat the oil over medium heat. Add the onion and cook for 5 minutes, or until softened, stirring occasionally.

2. Add the sugar and cook for 5 minutes more, or until the onion starts to caramelize.

3. Remove the onion to a plate and add the mushrooms, garlic, and ½ teaspoon of the salt to the pot. Cook for 3 minutes, or until the liquid from the mushrooms starts to evaporate. Remove the mushrooms to the plate with the onion and set aside.

4. Add the chicken broth and bring to a boil. Add the barley and the remaining ½ teaspoon salt, reduce the heat to low, cover, and cook for 45 minutes, or until tender. (Using just the one pot helps the flavors to combine.)

5. Stir in the onion and mushrooms, cook until heated through, and serve.

kiddie slaw

My kids are obsessed with slaws. I'm not sure if it's because they find the tiny pieces of veggies so easy to chew or because they like the tangy dressing, but whatever it is, it works!

1. Combine the yogurt, mayonnaise, mustard, honey, and salt in a large bowl.

2. Using a hand grater or the grater attachment on your food processor, grate the cabbage, carrots, and bell pepper.

3. Add the grated vegetables to the bowl with the dressing, toss to coat, and serve. The slaw will taste great kept for a couple of days in the fridge.

4 servings

¼ cup Greek yogurt

1 tablespoon mayonnaise

1 tablespoon Dijon mustard

1 tablespoon honey

¼ teaspoon salt

½ Napa cabbage

2 medium carrots

1 red bell pepper, seeded and quartered

black bean cakes

One 15-ounce can black beans, rinsed and drained

Kernels from 1 ear of corn, or 1 cup frozen kernels, defrosted

½ cup shredded Cheddar cheese

¼ cup packed chopped cilantro

¼ teaspoon garlic powder

¼ teaspoon onion powder

2 tablespoons bread crumbs

1 large egg

Vegetable or canola oil, for cooking

ACCOMPANIMENTS

Big Kid Guacamole (page 110) or sour cream

My kids love to eat black beans with brown rice, in quesadillas, or even on their own. As delicious as black beans are in their natural state, it's still fun to transform them into something entirely different.

Beans are an incredible source of fiber and iron, and because of their soft texture they're perfect for forming into these little cakelike patties. Sometimes I find it hard to come up with yummy vegetarian recipes that are truly filling, but these totally fit the bill.

I like to serve these Black Bean Cakes with a little guacamole and sour cream on the side as dips. The only real problem I have making this recipe is keeping my husband away from them. He can eat an entire batch in one sitting. Luckily most of the ingredients are things I keep on hand, so I can quickly cook up more for us to have at dinner and to munch on throughout the next day.

1. Place all the ingredients except the oil in a food processor and puree (it's fine if the puree has a few little chunks).

2. Heat the oil in a large sauté pan over medium heat.

3. Place 1 tablespoon of the bean mixture in the pan. Using the back of a spoon, spread the mixture into an even circle. Repeat to fill the pan with patties, keeping a bit of room between each.

4. Cook for 3 minutes, flip onto the other side, and cook for another 3 to 4 minutes, until cooked through. It is very important to be patient and cook the patties a full 3 minutes before flipping or they may break apart. Set the patties aside when they are done.

5. Cook the remaining patties, adding 1 tablespoon of oil for each batch.

6. Serve with your desired accompaniments.

TO FREEZE: *Transfer the cooled patties to a zip-top bag, label, and freeze for up to 4 months. When ready to cook, heat them in a 300°F oven for a few minute; if you take them straight from the freezer, heat them for 10 minutes.*

📺 spinach gnocchi

40 small gnocchi balls

One 10-ounce package frozen chopped spinach, defrosted

1 cup full-fat ricotta cheese

⅔ cup grated Parmesan cheese, plus 2 tablespoons for sprinkling

1 large egg yolk

2 tablespoons all-purpose flour, plus more for dusting your hands while rolling

This is a scrumptious eat-with-your-hands recipe that's great for all ages but especially for all those little ones yet to have teeth. The inspiration for it came from the many conversations I had with parents whose twelve-, thirteen-, or even fourteen-month-olds were still toothless. They really wanted to move their tykes beyond purees but needed a recipe soft enough for them to chew (or gum).

Popeye would be proud of this recipe. Packed with spinach and creamy ricotta, these little morsels are like delicate soft pillows and so easy to make. You can serve them with a little red sauce, but for easier cleanup, I highly recommend just a little sprinkle of Parmesan, and that's it!

1. Squeeze all of the water out of the spinach using your hands (do it in small handfuls over a bowl to make sure you don't lose any spinach) and then again in a clean dish towel to remove as much liquid as possible (see Note).

2. Place the spinach, ricotta cheese, ⅔ cup of the Parmesan cheese, the egg yolk, and 2 tablespoons flour in a food processor and pulse until the spinach is in tiny pieces and the mixture is thoroughly combined.

3. Dust your hands with a little flour so the mixture doesn't stick to your hands.

4. Take 1 teaspoon of the spinach mixture and roll it into a tiny ball. Place it on a plate covered with parchment paper. Repeat with the rest of the mixture.

5. Bring a large pot of water to a boil. Add the gnocchi in small batches—no more than several at a time—and cook for 3 minutes, or until they rise to the surface.

6. Using a slotted spoon, remove the gnocchi to a plate or bowl.

7. Sprinkle with Parmesan cheese and serve.

NOTE: *This recipe will not succeed unless you remove all of the water from the spinach so that it's as dry as possible (see page 221 for how). If you do not drain the spinach well, the gnocchi will fall apart while cooking in the water.*

TO FREEZE: *After step 4, place the gnocchi on a baking sheet and freeze for 30 minutes. Transfer to a zip-top bag, label, and freeze for up to 4 months. When ready to cook, thaw to room temperature and start at step 5.*

baked zucchini coins

I once did a poll on the weelicious Facebook page asking parents what their kids' favorite green vegetables were. While broccoli and peas ranked high on the list, zucchini was barely mentioned. Maybe that's because people aren't familiar with how to prepare it. A lot of people steam zucchini, which I find makes it a bit limp and lifeless, and I can understand why kids don't take to a vegetable with that kind of texture. Since I'm always playing around with fun new ways to prepare vegetables that kids can be excited to eat, I decided to revisit zucchini.

Zucchini has a very delicate flavor, so I focused on a simple preparation. These zucchini coins are baked, which makes them crunchy on the outside and soft and tender inside—a real textural treat for kids (and Kenya gets a kick out of eating "coins" because he feels like he's got edible pocket change on his plate). Add a little tomato sauce on the side and they're the perfect side dish for your family to enjoy with any meal.

1. Preheat the oven to 450°F.

2. Combine the panko, Parmesan, salt, and garlic powder in a small bowl. Whisk the egg in a second bowl and place the flour in a third bowl.

3. Make an assembly line with the bowls. Dip the zucchini coins first into the flour, then the egg, and last into the panko mixture, coating evenly and repeating with the remaining zucchini coins.

4. Place the coins on a baking rack set over a baking sheet, coat them with cooking spray, and bake for 20 minutes, or until the panko is golden.

5. Serve with tomato sauce, if desired.

TO FREEZE: *After step 3, place the coins on a baking sheet and freeze for 30 minutes. Place them in a zip-top bag, label, and freeze for up to 3 months. When ready to eat, remove them from the freezer and start at step 4, adding at least 3 to 5 minutes to the baking time.*

4 servings

½ cup whole wheat panko or bread crumbs

¼ cup grated Parmesan cheese

½ teaspoon salt

½ teaspoon garlic powder

1 large egg

¼ cup all-purpose flour

2 medium zucchini, cut into ¼-inch coins

Olive or canola oil cooking spray

Optional: weelicious Tomato Sauce (page 116) or marinara sauce, for dipping

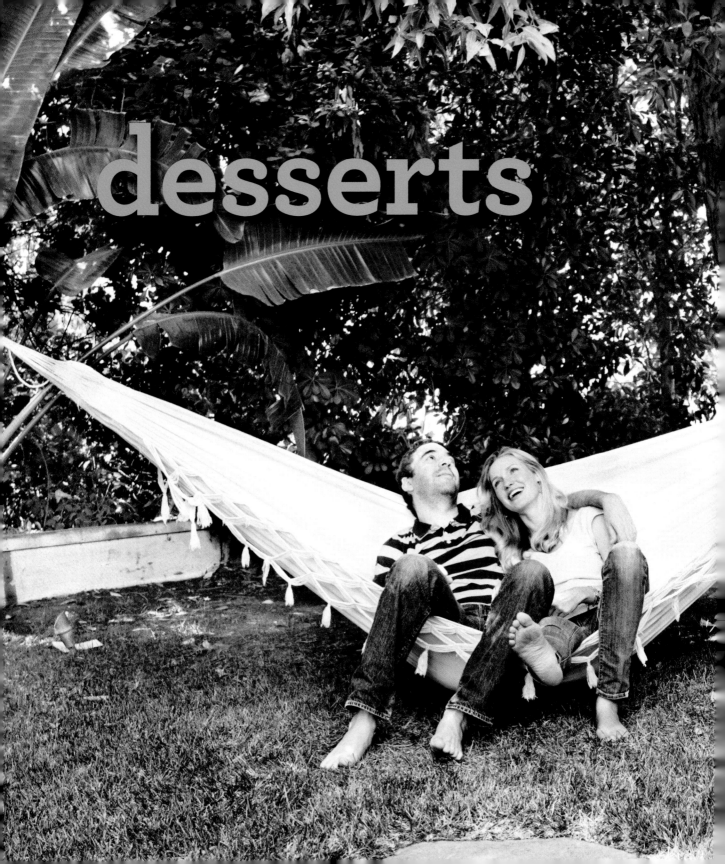

desserts

raspberry–cream cheese heart tarts

about 10 tarts

½ cup fresh or defrosted frozen raspberries

¼ cup whipped cream cheese

1 tablespoon honey or agave nectar

1 Double Pie Crust (recipe follows) or one 14-ounce premade pie crust

ICING

10 fresh or defrosted frozen raspberries

1 tablespoon milk or water

1½ cups powdered sugar

I'm one of those people who loves everything about Valentine's Day (you may be saying "blech" right now, but I do). Well, I'm not particularly fond of how commercial the holiday has become, but I do love all the hugs, kisses, homemade cards, and, of course, sweet treats! While you can easily buy your Valentine a bag of SweeTarts with cute sayings printed on them, why not go to the store, buy some fresh ingredients, and make something special with your kids instead? This year, Kenya, Chloe, and I made Raspberry–Cream Cheese Heart Tarts for Daddy to show him just how much we love him. After all, isn't food the best way to a daddy's heart?

Pop-Tarts were a childhood favorite of mine, and this is my healthier spin on them. They're filled with fresh raspberries, and the pink icing is made with raspberry juice rather than food coloring. If Pop-Tarts had actually been made this way, I might have gotten to eat them more often as a kid.

These are an unbelievably easy and deliciously fun way to share the love with those most special to you. Just wait till you try them—they'll make a Valentine's Day lover out of you yet!

1. Place the raspberries, cream cheese, and honey in a bowl. Using the back of a fork, mash the raspberries with the cream cheese, leaving some pieces of raspberry intact.

TAMARA: My little girl and I made Raspberry–Cream Cheese Heart Tarts for one of our first baking sessions. What a wonderful and yummy way to enjoy time together, and their heart shape was a perfect visual for the fun and love that day!

2. Roll out the pie crust to ¼ inch thick and, using a heart-shaped cookie cutter about the size of your fist, cut out about 20 heart shapes.

3. Place 1 heart on a lightly floured work surface and place 2 teaspoons of the cream cheese mixture in the center, leaving a ¼-inch border.

4. Lightly dip your index finger into a cup of water and "brush" the border with water. This will allow the 2 sides of the heart to adhere to each other.

5. Top with another cutout heart. With the tines of a fork, gently press down along the edges to adhere the 2 sides, making sure not to press so hard that the cream cheese mixture goes beyond the boundary of the pastry heart. With a toothpick, poke some holes in the top of the heart to remove any air pockets.

6. Repeat to make the rest of the heart tarts.

7. Preheat the oven to 400°F.

8. Place the tarts on a parchment- or Silpat-lined baking sheet and bake for 20 minutes, or until golden. Set the tarts aside to cool.

9. While the hearts are baking, make the icing. Place the raspberries in a strainer and press down with the back of a spoon to release the raspberry juice into a bowl. You should have about 2 tablespoons of juice.

10. Whisk in the milk and slowly whisk in the powdered sugar.

11. When the tarts are cool, use a spoon to spread the raspberry icing over the hearts and serve.

KELLY: My friend Amy made the Raspberry–Cream Cheese Heart Tarts for our stroller strides Valentine's Day party, and they were a huge hit with the kids and moms alike!

KIMBERLY: I bought all of the ingredients for your Raspberry–Cream Cheese Heart Tarts, intending to make them for my sons to eat on Valentine's Day morning. Life intervened, and I didn't have the time to make them. A couple of days later I realized that I needed to make them ASAP or the raspberries were going to go bad. My husband had his army buddies over for a poker game that night, so I ended up making the heart tarts for them. They were a huge hit. Even the guys who said that they didn't normally like cream cheese loved them.

TO FREEZE: *After step 6, place the hearts on a baking sheet and freeze for 1 hour. Place the hearts in a zip-top bag, label, and freeze for up to 3 months. To bake, start at step 7, adding an extra 3 minutes to the baking time.*

📺 double pie crust

1. Place the butter, shortening, flour, and salt in a food processor and pulse until the mixture resembles coarse cornmeal.

2. Sprinkle 1 tablespoon of the ice water in the food processor at a time and pulse a few times, until the dough starts to come together.

3. Place the dough on a piece of parchment or plastic wrap, gather it into a ball, and flatten it into a disk.

4. Refrigerate the dough for 30 minutes, or until chilled.

5. Proceed with your recipe. The dough will keep for up to 1 week in the refrigerator or up to 2 months in the freezer.

MEGAN: I made the Raspberry–Cream Cheese Heart Tarts for my family for Valentine's Day. The kids were so excited about their homemade Pop Tarts, and my hubby and I enjoyed a couple with our morning coffee as well. Huge hit!

1 double crust

½ cup (1 stick) unsalted butter, chilled and cubed

½ cup vegetable shortening or lard, chilled and cubed

2 ½ cups all-purpose flour

1 teaspoon salt

5 to 6 tablespoons ice water

1 tablespoon honey

carrot-pineapple cupcakes with cream cheese icing

14 cupcakes

1½ cups all-purpose flour

¾ teaspoon baking powder

¾ teaspoon baking soda

½ teaspoon salt

½ teaspoon ground cinnamon

¾ cup honey or agave nectar

½ cup vegetable oil

2 large eggs

1½ cups peeled and grated carrots

¼ cup drained crushed pineapple

Cream Cheese Icing (recipe follows)

Birthday parties for little ones can be loads of fun, but the last thing a parent wants on the ride home is their kid on a sugar high from all the birthday cake. These carrot cupcakes are delectable and a little bit different from the norm, as they're made with honey or agave nectar instead of white sugar.

When it comes to cooking with sweeteners, I'm all about balance and variety in what I use. One example is using agave nectar, a sweet plant-based liquid that's similar to honey. It's low on the glycemic index and is metabolized by your body more slowly than sugar, so it has a less severe effect on blood sugar fluctuations. It's easily found in stores these days, and I'll bet you'll find a number of ways for it to replace white sugar in your kitchen.

For birthdays, instead of baking one big cake, I prefer to decorate a platter with a bunch of cupcakes and put toppings on the side. Kids love to decorate their own little cakes with nuts, sprinkles, or whatever suits their fancy. It's also a good way to offer portion control. Anyway, these cupcakes are a blast to make for any special occasion and heavenly tasting to eat!

1. Preheat the oven to 350°F and line 14 muffin cups with paper liners.

2. Sift the flour, baking powder, baking soda, salt, and cinnamon into a medium bowl.

3. In a separate bowl or a standing mixer, beat the agave, oil, and eggs until thoroughly combined.

4. Slowly mix the dry ingredients into the wet ingredients.

5. Add the carrots and pineapple and stir until all the ingredients are thoroughly combined.

6. Scoop the batter into muffin cups, filling them three quarters full.

7. Bake for about 30 minutes for regular cupcakes (15 minutes for mini cupcakes), or until a toothpick inserted into the center of a cupcake comes out clean. Cool thoroughly. The cupcakes can be made 1 day ahead, covered, and stored at room temperature.

8. Spread the top of each cupcake with 2 tablespoons of cream cheese icing (1 teaspoon for a mini cupcake) and serve.

cream cheese icing

1. Place all the ingredients in a mixer and beat on medium to high speed until light and fluffy.

2. Spread on the cupcakes.

EMMA: It was my daughter Quin's first birthday, and getting her to eat food was near impossible—she choked and gagged at any texture but a completely smooth puree. I decided to make the Carrot-Pineapple Cupcakes with Cream Cheese Icing for everyone else, if not for her. I spent two days baking and shaping them so I could turn them into cake pops using the icing to bind them, and they were adorable! At the party we were all gathered for a photo holding our cake pops, including Quin. I set the camera on self timer and ran to stand beside Quin, and just as the camera flashed she took a giant bite of her cupcake! She chewed it, swallowed, and went in for more, finishing the entire thing! From that moment Quin's made incredible progress with food, and today she's a two-year-old with the palate of a seasoned foodie! That cupcake literally changed her life.

2 cups

One 8-ounce package cream cheese, softened

½ cup (1 stick) unsalted butter, softened

¼ cup honey or agave nectar

1 teaspoon pure vanilla extract

banana bread cake

When I first got really excited about cooking as a kid, one of the first recipes I made was banana bread. It's super-simple to make, extremely forgiving if your proportions are slightly off, and nutritious to boot. Whenever I have spotty bananas sitting around the kitchen, I make this spin on my original recipe. It's a real special treat that is lighter and much less dense—more like a cake than traditional banana bread.

1. Preheat the oven to 350°F and coat an 8 x 8-inch baking dish with cooking spray.

2. Place 2 of the bananas, the eggs, milk, oats, vanilla, brown sugar, and butter in a blender and puree for 1 minute (it's okay if there are pieces of oat remaining in the batter).

3. In a separate bowl, whisk the flour, baking powder, baking soda, and salt.

4. Slowly pour the dry ingredients into the wet ingredients and stir to combine. If you're adding nuts, stir them in now.

5. Pour the batter into the baking dish. Slice the remaining 2 bananas lengthwise to make 10 long banana strips and layer them on top to cover the batter.

6. Lightly sprinkle ground cinnamon on top of the banana slices and bake for 40 to 45 minutes, until a toothpick comes out clean.

7. Serve right away or cool and slice and serve with a nice cup of herbal tea—kids will enjoy it, too!

6 to 8 servings

Olive or canola oil cooking spray

4 ripe bananas, peeled

2 large eggs

½ cup milk

½ cup old-fashioned (not instant and not steel-cut) oats

1 teaspoon pure vanilla extract

½ cup packed brown sugar

6 tablespoons (¾ stick) unsalted butter, melted

1 cup all-purpose flour

1 teaspoon baking powder

½ teaspoon baking soda

¼ teaspoon salt

½ cup chopped walnuts or pecans (optional)

Ground cinnamon, to sprinkle on top

chocolate rice crisp-wee treats

16 triangles, squares, or balls

Olive or canola oil cooking spray

⅔ cup brown rice syrup

⅓ cup smooth peanut butter

⅓ cup smooth almond butter

¼ cup cocoa powder

3 ½ cups crispy rice cereal

I'm sure your kids have tried rice crispy treats, but have they ever had a *chocolate* rice crispy treat? Unlike the ones you would buy at the grocery made with lots of corn syrup, these get their sweet taste from brown rice syrup and some added nutrition from high-protein peanut and almond butters. Now, those treats that you may have avoided in the past may actually become something you'll be more than happy to give your little ones.

1. Coat an 8 x 8-inch baking dish with cooking spray.

2. In a large saucepan over low heat, whisk the brown rice syrup, peanut butter, almond butter, and cocoa powder for about 2 minutes, until melted and starting to bubble.

3. Place the rice cereal in a large bowl, pour in the nut butter mixture, and stir with a spatula until completely combined.

4. Pour the mixture into the pan and press down to flatten the top (I put my hand in a zip-top bag to keep it from sticking).

5. Cool for 5 minutes, then cut into triangle shapes or squares or roll into balls, and serve.

chocolate–peanut butter pudding

2 servings

1 cup plain Greek yogurt

2 tablespoons cocoa powder

2 tablespoons smooth peanut butter

3 tablespoons honey or agave nectar

The flavor combination of chocolate and peanut butter is an all-time classic, and Kenya loves it, so why not create my own special treat with them? Not wanting to go too overboard, I tried to figure out how to add at least *some* nutritional value to such a decadent treat. I started with a base of Greek yogurt, and with just a few additional ingredients produced a thick, rich pudding that made Kenya's and Chloe's eyes bug out when they saw it. You'd think they couldn't have been any more excited, but you should have seen the looks on their faces when they tasted it. Heaven.

Place all the ingredients in a food processor or blender, pulse to combine, and serve. The pudding will keep in the fridge for up to 3 days.

fruit and oat bars

Whenever I'm working on recipes for weelicious, my husband relishes his role as one of my most skilled taste testers. He, Kenya, and Chloe, seated side by side, will offer me their "oohs and aahhs" when I've nailed it and the occasional thumbs down (how dare they?!) when I don't meet their high standards.

When I set off to create this recipe, I knew the challenge was going to be whether I could keep the bars moist and healthy. On the first try, with a slightly different recipe and cooking time, the crust was a bit too dry (my husband disagreed and declared them a masterpiece). On the second try, with a few tweaks, I came up with this version, which still satisfied hubby and is also yummy and perfect for kids' school lunch boxes.

These bars are one of our family's favorite recipes. For me, it's because they're healthy and packed with fiber and other nutrients, and they're sweet without all the sugar and junk you'll find in a store-bought equivalent. For the rest of my family, it's because they're just so darn good.

1. Preheat the oven to 350°F and coat an 11 x 7-inch pan with cooking spray.

2. Place all the ingredients except the apple butter in a food processor. Pulse until the ingredients are combined and the oats and nuts are in small pieces.

3. Press down all but 1 cup of the mixture into the bottom of the pan.

4. Spread the oat mixture thoroughly with the apple butter.

5. Crumble the remaining 1 cup of the oat mixture over the apple butter.

6. Bake for 30 to 35 minutes, until golden.

7. Cool, cut, and serve. The bars will keep in the fridge for up to 3 days.

18 bars

Olive or canola oil cooking spray

2 cups old-fashioned oats (not instant and not steel-cut)

1 cup all-purpose flour

2 tablespoons wheat germ

½ teaspoon baking soda

½ cup (1 stick) plus 2 tablespoons unsalted butter

⅓ cup chopped nuts— almonds, cashews, peanuts, and/or walnuts

¼ cup honey or agave nectar

2 cups apple butter, or one 10- to 12-ounce jar fruit preserves

chocolate velvet beet cupcakes

14 cupcakes

⅓ cup cocoa powder

1½ cups all-purpose flour

2 teaspoons baking powder

½ teaspoon baking soda

¾ cup sugar

½ teaspoon salt

2 large eggs

1 cup milk

⅓ cup vegetable or canola oil

1 large beet, roasted, cooled, peeled, and pureed (about ¾ cup) (see To Puree Beets)

2 teaspoons pure vanilla extract

Cream Cheese Frosting (recipe follows)

Now and then, we love taking the kids by our favorite neighborhood cupcake store to enjoy a special treat. Of course their eyes are always drawn to the most colorful cupcakes in the display case. My kids may have no idea how they actually taste, but put something like a red velvet cupcake made with crimson food dye in front of them and their immediate response is, "That one." These chocolate velvet cupcakes have a rich chocolate flavor, but they aren't artificially red like cupcakes that use chemical food dyes. They and their icing get their bright reddish-pink color from a surprising, delicious, and 100% natural guest: roasted beets. You'd never know that though, since there's no beet flavor in them. Just deep, rich chocolate!

I offer two ingredient versions for the frosting here, one white and one a delightful beet-stained pink!

1. Preheat the oven to 350°F.

2. Sift the cocoa powder, flour, baking powder, baking soda, sugar, and salt into a large bowl.

3. In a separate bowl, whisk together the rest of the ingredients.

4. Slowly add the dry ingredients to the wet, stirring to combine thoroughly as you go.

5. Pour about ⅓ cup batter into paper-lined muffin cups and bake for 25 minutes, or until a toothpick comes out clean.

6. Cool thoroughly, frost, and serve. The cupcakes will keep in a covered container on the counter for 1 day, or in the fridge for up to 3 days, or you can freeze them for up to 3 months.

TO PUREE BEETS: *Preheat the oven to 375°F. Wrap the beets in foil and bake for 45 minutes, or until fork-tender. Remove the beets from the foil and set aside until cool to the touch. Put your hand in a zip-top bag (to avoid staining your hand) and rub the skins from the beets. Puree the beets until smooth.*

cream cheese frosting

1. Place all the ingredients in a mixer and beat on medium-high speed until fluffy.

2. Spread the frosting onto the cooled cupcakes.

½ cups

FOR WHITE FROSTING

One 8-ounce package cream cheese, at room temperature

½ cup (1 stick) unsalted butter, at room temperature

¼ cup powdered sugar

1 teaspoon pure vanilla extract

FOR PINK FROSTING

One 8-ounce package cream cheese, at room temperature

½ cup (1 stick) unsalted butter, at room temperature

½ cup powdered sugar

1 medium beet, roasted, cooled, peeled, and pureed (about ½ cup) (see page 244)

1 teaspoon pure vanilla extract

sweet beet cookies

1 cup all-purpose flour

**½ teaspoon baking
powder**

2 tablespoons sugar

¼ teaspoon salt

**1 fresh medium beet
(not canned)**

**2 tablespoons canola
or vegetable oil**

"I don't like beets!" That was my darling son's response when I told him I had made Sweet Beet Cookies. I thought sandwiching the word "beet" between "sweet" and "cookie" would add sufficient appeal for Kenya. Not so much.

But if the name itself wasn't a selling point, the mere sight of these cookies was. When Kenya finally saw them, his eyes lit up. "They're beautiful," he said. "I love beets!" They're the kind of treats that make *everyone* happy. Beet that!

1. Preheat the oven to 400°F.

2. Place the flour, baking powder, sugar, and salt in a large bowl and stir to combine.

3. Use a knife or vegetable peeler to peel the beet, taking care not to stain everything in sight with red beet juice. Shred the peeled beet using a fine Microplane grater.

4. Add ½ cup of the shredded beet to the flour mixture. Use your hands to coat the beet pieces with the flour.

5. Add the oil and work with your hands to bring the dough together. Knead the dough for 2 to 3 minutes, or until a smooth dough is formed.

6. Form the dough into a flat rectangular disk and roll it out ¼ inch thick on parchment paper or a clean, dry surface.

7. Using a knife, cut the dough into squares, or use small cookie cutters to cut it into shapes.

8. Bake the cookies on a Silpat- or parchment-lined cookie sheet for 15 to 17 minutes, until firm to the touch.

9. Cool and serve. These cookies are best stored on the counter in an airtight container.

banana–oat–chocolate chip cookies

30 cookies

3 very ripe bananas

2 cups old-fashioned oats (not instant and not steel-cut)

1 cup pitted and chopped dried Medjool dates

¼ cup canola or vegetable oil

½ teaspoon ground cinnamon

¼ teaspoon salt

½ cup chocolate chips

Is it really possible to have a cookie recipe that *doesn't* call for any sugar, butter, or flour but *still* produces cookies that are just as sweet and delicious as the ones you're normally used to eating? Well, not only are these treats incredibly easy to make—even for moms who rarely bake—they're also pretty nutritious (totally nutritious if you leave out the chocolate chips) and tons of fun for kids to help make.

When I whip these up with my son, he totally gets into it by helping me smash the bananas and toss the ingredients into the mixing bowl . . . and then by trying to eat as much of the dough as he possibly can before it hits the cookie sheet! As there are no eggs in this recipe, I don't worry about letting him stuff himself. After all, you only get to be a kid once, and eating cookie dough is part of the fun of baking!

P.S. You have to freeze a few of these. The kids go crazy for them right out of the freezer.

JULEY: Your Banana–Oat–Chocolate Chip Cookies have been a lifesaver for me. My doctor put me on a gluten-free diet, and I've lived off these cookies for my dessert this past year. I usually substitute walnuts for the chocolate chips and sometimes throw in some flax seeds, but they always turn out great and satisfy my sweet tooth!

1. Preheat the oven to 350°F.

2. Mash the bananas in a bowl. Add the remaining ingredients and mix well.

3. Allow the mixture to sit for 10 minutes.

4. Using a mini ice cream scoop or tablespoon, scoop out the dough onto a Silpat- or parchment-lined baking sheet. (To make bars instead of cookies, place the dough in a 7 x 11-inch dish sprayed with cooking spray, bake for 35 to 40 minutes, until golden, and allow to cool. Cut into bars or squares.)

5. Bake for 25 minutes, or until golden.

6. Cool and serve.

TO FREEZE: *Cool the cookies thoroughly, place in a zip-top bag, label, and freeze for up to 3 months. They're delicious eaten straight out of the freezer.*

TIP: *To turn these into a breakfast cookie (yes, a breakfast cookie!), replace the chocolate chips with walnuts or raisins.*

SHANNON: We *loooove* the Banana–Oat–Chocolate Chip Cookies because they're naturally sweet and yummy without lots of sugar or preservatives. It's such a quick, easy recipe that my four-year-old and I can make it together.

pb&j oatmeal thumbprint cookies

about 60 cookies

1½ cups all-purpose flour

1 teaspoon baking soda

½ teaspoon salt

1 cup old-fashioned oats (not instant and not steel-cut)

½ cup (1 stick) unsalted butter, softened

½ cup honey or agave nectar

1 large egg

1 teaspoon pure vanilla extract

1 cup smooth peanut butter

About ⅔ cup jam, jelly, or preserves of your choice

Wanting to improve on yet another childhood memory that's still vivid in my mind, I came up with these cookies. I've re-created many of my unhealthy childhood favorites in this book, only as healthy versions. What strikes me is how easy it is to make healthy desserts your kids will love without sacrificing taste. Instead of the hydrogenated fats and untold amounts of sugar that comprised the thumbprint cookies I ate as a kid every Sunday after church, I added naturally sweet honey, fiber-packed oats, and protein-rich peanut butter, then topped them off with fresh preserves for a tasty real fruit touch.

My kids were so excited when I put these fresh baked cookies in front of them, but the best part was watching Kenya react just as his mommy used to: by digging out the preserves first.

1. Preheat the oven to 350°F.

2. In a large bowl, combine the flour, baking soda, salt, and oats.

3. In a large bowl or standing mixer, beat the butter and honey for 1 minute on medium speed.

4. Add the egg, vanilla, and peanut butter and beat 1 minute more, or until smooth.

5. Slowly add the dry ingredients to the wet, mixing to incorporate as you go.

6. Drop the cookie dough 1 tablespoon at a time onto Silpat- or parchment-lined baking sheets and use your thumb or index finger to make an indentation in the center of each cookie.

7. Fill each indentation with about ½ teaspoon of jam, jelly, or preserves.

8. Bake for 10 to 12 minutes, until firm.

9. Cool on baking racks and serve. The cookies will keep in a covered container on the counter for up to 2 days or in the fridge for up to 1 week.

apple-walnut cookies

I've gotten into the habit of baking a dozen or so cookies to eat now and then freezing what remains for another day. Whether you're having a dinner party, last-minute guests, or just want a spur-of-the-moment treat, always having homemade cookies on hand—instead of a box of store-bought cookies that will be stale within a week—is just about the coziest thing ever.

1. Preheat the oven to 350°F.

2. In a large bowl, combine the flours, oats, baking soda, baking powder, salt, and cinnamon.

3. Using a standing mixer or hand mixer, beat the butter and honey on medium speed for 1 minute, or until creamy.

4. Add the egg and vanilla and beat on medium speed until smooth, about 1 minute.

5. Slowly add the dry ingredients to the wet, mixing to incorporate as you go.

6. Stir the apple and walnuts into the batter.

7. Drop 1 tablespoon of dough at a time onto a Silpat- or parchment-lined cookie sheet, keeping space between the cookies.

8. Bake for 12 minutes, or until golden.

9. Remove to a cooling rack and serve.

TIP: *Using a small ice cream scooper instead of a spoon is an easy way to make your cookies.*

TO FREEZE: *At step 7, freeze the cookie dough on the baking sheet for 1 hour, then place the balls in zip-top bags, label, and store for up to 3 months. When ready to bake, place the frozen cookie balls on a baking sheet and add 1 minute to the baking time.*

4 dozen cookies

½ cup whole wheat flour

1½ cups all-purpose flour

⅓ cup old-fashioned oats

1 teaspoon baking soda

1 teaspoon baking powder

½ teaspoon salt

1 teaspoon ground cinnamon

½ cup (1 stick) unsalted butter, softened

⅔ cup honey or agave nectar

1 large egg

1 teaspoon pure vanilla extract

1 apple, peeled, cored, and diced into small cubes (about 1 cup)

1 cup chopped walnuts

carrot cake cookies

3 dozen cookies

1½ cups all-purpose flour

½ cup old-fashioned oats (not instant and not steel-cut)

1 teaspoon ground cinnamon

1 teaspoon baking powder

½ teaspoon baking soda

½ teaspoon salt

½ cup (1 stick) unsalted butter, softened

¾ cup packed brown sugar

1 large egg

1 teaspoon pure vanilla extract

1 cup finely shredded carrot (from about 2 large peeled carrots)

½ cup chopped walnuts

When I'm coming up with new recipes, I always try to keep my fruit and veggie hat on. I want my kids to get as many nutritious foods as possible into their bodies, even when they're eating cookies (or should I say *especially* when they're eating cookies). My mother made the most scrumptious carrot cake when I was growing up, but her recipe takes a lot of time. This is my *much* faster and easier version of her carrot cake, but I made it as a cookie, since it helps me manage portion control with the kids. Full of vitamin-rich carrots, nuts, and oats, these cookies are soft, tender, and sweet, and while I wouldn't necessarily call this health food, compared to most cookies they keep a bit of the guilt at bay.

1. Preheat the oven to 350°F.

2. Combine the flour, oats, cinnamon, baking powder, baking soda, and salt in a large bowl.

3. Beat the butter and sugar in a large bowl or standing mixer for 2 minutes on medium speed.

4. Add the egg and vanilla and beat for 1 minute more, or until smooth.

5. Slowly add the dry ingredients to the wet, mixing to combine as you go.

6. Stir the carrots and walnuts into the batter.

7. Drop the cookie dough 1 tablespoon at a time onto Silpat- or parchment-lined cookie sheets and flatten the dough a bit with your finger.

8. Bake for 12 minutes, or until golden.

9. Cool on baking racks and serve. The cookies will keep in a covered container on the counter for up to 1 day or up to 3 days in the fridge.

TIP: *To make these cookies even more exciting and carrot cake-like, create a simple frosting for them: Place some softened or whipped cream cheese in a bowl with a little bit of honey or sugar, whisk to combine, and spread on the cooled cookies. You could even sandwich them with that filling to make carrot cake whoopie pies.*

honey-cinnamon cookies

I originally made these for my kids as a holiday treat, but they loved them so much that I now double the recipe and keep a roll of the dough in the freezer so they can enjoy homemade slice 'n bake cookies anytime.

   The dough needs to rest in the refrigerator for 2 hours after mixing, so do plan ahead!

1. In a large bowl, whisk together the flour, baking soda, salt, cinnamon, and ginger.

2. Beat the butter, brown sugar, and honey in a standing mixer (or in a bowl using a hand beater) for 1 minute on medium speed, or until smooth and creamy.

3. Add the egg and beat for 1 minute.

4. Slowly add the dry ingredients to the wet ingredients, mixing as you go.

5. Shape the dough into a log, cover with plastic wrap, and refrigerate for at least 2 hours or up to 2 days.

6. Preheat the oven to 400°F.

7. Cut the cookies into ½-inch slices and place them on Silpat- or parchment-lined baking sheets. Bake for 10 to 12 minutes, until golden.

8. Cool on baking racks and serve.

TO FREEZE: *After step 5, the wrapped cookie log can be frozen for up to 3 months. When you're ready to bake, continue from step 6.*

30 cookies

- 2 ½ cups all-purpose flour
- ½ teaspoon baking soda
- ½ teaspoon salt
- 1 teaspoon ground cinnamon
- ¼ teaspoon ground ginger
- ½ cup (1 stick) unsalted butter, softened
- ½ cup packed brown sugar
- ⅓ cup honey
- 1 large egg

drinks

LINDSEY: We love the Spooky Smoothie! My littlest, three-year-old Jonathan, loves to help peel the bananas and grab fistfuls of spinach to drop in the blender. The excitement on his face as the smoothie turns green is priceless, and I love that I'm not having to sneak vegetables into my kids' diets. They know exactly what they're drinking! My daughter, Allison, likes to help come up with new concoctions. To make this even more nutritious, I usually add some flax seed oil and a handful of frozen wild blueberries. Of course, the smoothie is no longer green, but the kids don't mind, and I'm one happy mama watching them slurp down their drink!

NANCY: I'm in charge of setting up all the cooking projects for our co-op preschool class. I was looking for a green drink for St. Patrick's Day, and we made Green Monster Smoothies. The kids had fun making them, it was easy to clean up, and some kids who were averse to green foods tried them, loved them, and asked their parents to make them at home!

green monster smoothie

I'm pretty lucky to have kids who eat their greens. But even if I didn't, I'm pretty sure this Green Monster Smoothie would be irresistible to them. I came up with the name because it's a monster of nutrition and it's so delicious, it's scary. If you have a kid who avoids eating greens, this drink treat just may be the answer to your prayers.

On a vegetable nutrition ranking, spinach is way up at the top in terms of vitamin and mineral richness—there's no doubt why Popeye ate so much of the stuff. It gives this delicious drink a beautiful green color as well as a mild, sweet flavor that will surprise you. This smoothie packs a lot of goodness and yumminess into one glass.

1. Place all the ingredients in a blender and puree until smooth.

2. Serve with a tall straw to slurp it up.

4 servings

2 cups vanilla rice milk

4 cups packed fresh spinach

2 large ripe bananas

1 tablespoon honey or agave nectar

LEE ANN: I make the Green Monster Smoothie all the time. My three-year-old son calls it a Spinach Mookshake. My kids get excited now when they see me putting spinach in the cart at the grocery store!

avocado shake

2 servings

1 ripe avocado, peeled and pitted

1 cup cow's milk, rice milk, or almond milk (more for a thinner shake)

1 large ripe banana

1 large handful of ice

I was a bit surprised when I discovered that in Brazil and other South American countries, avocados are used primarily in sweet dishes, such as ice cream and dessert mousses. In the United States, we're much more accustomed to avocados popping up in savory dishes like guacamole or sliced on a sandwich.

My kids are always game for making smoothies, and they love avocados. For this recipe, I let them help peel and break up the banana and pour the milk into the blender. This shake is such a cool and refreshing treat that within seconds after finishing the first glass, both my kids are clamoring for more.

This mean, green, vitamin-packed drink is the perfect sweet snack for any time of the day!

1. Place all the ingredients in a blender and puree.

2. Serve with a tall straw.

CHRISTINE: My girls *love* the Avocado Shake. Madeline is not too keen on trying new things, but since she helped me make the first one, she didn't hesitate at all to try it! Every day they get their chairs and bring them to the counter. Isabella used to just sit and watch us make them, but now she joins in the fun by adding the ice cubes to the blender. I've started freezing ripe avocados and very ripe bananas so I can keep up with the demand!

TESS: My one-year-old wakes up screaming with hunger every morning. I tried lots of different foods, but she would be too cranky to eat anything. Then I started making the Avocado Shake, and she was able to drink it quickly and cure her hunger with something delicious and nutritious.

MARGARET ANN: We make your Avocado Shake (dubbed the "monster milk shake") all the time! It's loved even by the non-avocado eaters at our house!

strawberr-wee lemonade

4 servings

1 cup hulled and chopped fresh strawberries

¼ cup honey or agave nectar

½ cup freshly squeezed lemon juice

Ice, for serving

Many of the Central and South American food stands at the Los Angeles farmers' markets feature huge, clear barrels of various naturally flavored lemonades. In addition to the tried-and-true original lemon version, there's also raspberry, strawberry, watermelon, and many other fresh combinations, their gorgeous colors luring anyone who passes by—my kids included.

These lemonades are made with a good deal of sugar, and so when possible, I try to steer Kenya and Chloe toward the fresh fruit displays instead, so we can make our own homemade Strawberr-Wee Lemonade. As soon as we unpack our farmers' market bounty, Kenya is up at the kitchen counter rolling the lemons (a kitchen job he loves, because he knows it's the best way to release the juice). With just a rinse of the berries, a touch of natural sweetener, a quick puree, and a brisk stir, our healthy lemonade is ready for us to gulp down and enjoy!

1. Puree the strawberries and honey in a blender or food processor until smooth and transfer to a pitcher.

2. Add 2 cups water and the lemon juice to the pitcher and stir to combine.

3. Chill and serve over ice.

veggie smoothie

I have enormous respect for moms who refuse to give in to the picky eater syndrome and continue to offer their kids vegetables in different forms until they find something that works. Juicing is a good option, but most moms I know don't own a juicer. I love making vegetable smoothies because they're packed with tons of vitamins and minerals, you get all the fiber, and you still have the great taste of the juice. And because you steam the veggies in this smoothie recipe before putting them in the blender, the end result is smooth, thick, and delicious!

1. Place the carrot and beet in a steamer pot over boiling water and cook for 8 minutes.

2. Add the cubed apple and cook for 2 minutes more.

3. Allow the vegetables and apple to cool, then place them in the blender with the juice.

4. Puree until smooth and serve.

2 servings

1 medium carrot, peeled and cut into 1-inch pieces (about ⅓ cup)

1 small beet, peeled and cut into 1-inch cubes (about ½ cup)

1 apple, peeled, cored, and cut into 1-inch cubes

1 cup apple or orange juice

blackberry agua fresca

4 servings

1½ cups fresh or frozen defrosted blackberries, rinsed

2 tablespoons honey or agave nectar

1 tablespoon lemon juice

I have a friend, Naomi, who is a total closet gourmet. While she couldn't be more humble about her culinary talents, just one taste of her food betrays how awesome she is in the kitchen. One time we ate dinner at her house and she served this incredibly delicious drink. It had a beautiful purple color, was unbelievably refreshing, and I had no idea what it was. She said it was an agua fresca. It sounded fancy, but she said it couldn't be easier to make. All she did was make a simple syrup of sugar and water, cut up some fresh ginger, and mix in frozen blackberries.

The next day, I set out to prepare an even simpler version for a group of kids coming over for a pool party. Kenya was ready as ever to be my taste tester as we took to the blender and whipped up a weelicious take on agua fresca.

When the kids arrived, I offered each of them a glass, asking, "Would you like to try some blackberry agua fresca?" The kids looked at me totally perplexed until their mothers leaned in and said, "It's juice." That's all it took. Within minutes it was all gone, with nothing left but purple mustaches on happy faces.

1. Place the blackberries, honey, and 4 cups water in a blender and puree.

2. Pour the blackberry mixture through a fine-mesh strainer into a pitcher.

3. Stir in the lemon juice, chill, and serve.

ginger-lemon-honey tea

The bane of every parent's existence: the common cold! Our house has been known to be a breeding ground for it. Kenya gets a cold, then I get it, then my husband, then Chloe, then Kenya again, and so it goes. Even the grandparents caught it over Thanksgiving one year.

I haven't found the cure, but I make this drink in abundance whenever the colds return. My husband and I have been drinking this potion for years and consider it to be a miracle for soothing a sore throat and clearing the head. And it's really yummy tasting. Ginger is used in Eastern medicine to treat bronchitis and other respiratory problems. Honey is fantastic for coating a sore throat, and lemon juice is packed with vitamin C.

This homeopathic remedy is a lifesaver! If you don't believe me, just ask Kenya, who asks for it even when he's not sick. It's really that delicious!

1. Cut the ginger into several thin disks.

2. Bring 2 cups of water and the ginger to a boil in a small saucepan over medium heat. Cover, reduce the heat to low, and cook for 5 to 10 minutes.

3. Remove the ginger from the water, add the lemon juice and honey, and stir to dissolve the honey.

4. Cool as needed for young kids, then serve the tea in mugs.

2 servings

1-inch piece of fresh ginger, peeled

Juice of 1 lemon

1 to 2 tablespoons honey, or to taste

cinnamon-honey milk

2 servings

2 cups milk (whole, skim, soy, almond, rice—any kind will work)

1 cinnamon stick or ½ teaspoon ground cinnamon

½ teaspoon pure vanilla extract

1 teaspoon honey

When I was little and couldn't sleep at night (or so I would declare to my parents to avoid going to bed), my parents would make me a glass of warm milk. I still love warm milk to this day, but here's my version of it, adding just a little more lovin'.

1. In a small saucepan, bring the milk, cinnamon, and vanilla to a simmer over low heat. Simmer for 10 minutes, but do not let it boil!

2. Remove from the heat and add the honey. Stir until the honey dissolves.

3. Cool as needed for young kids, then serve in mugs.

acknowledgments

First and foremost, this book would not exist were it not for the loyal and passionate readers who "stop by" the weelicious website every day. Your comments, suggestions, love of food, and concern about what you feed your families inspire me to create. You've been there for me from the very beginning, and I'm eternally grateful.

To the moms from *all over the world* who answered my call for help on Facebook and assisted in testing many of the recipes in this book, thank you for lending me your kitchens, time, resources, and families' palates. I'm so happy readers get to actually taste the invaluable contributions you made!

The weelicious website wasn't even two years old when I began working on the idea for this book. My committed book agent and now dear friend, Rebecca Oliver, believed in me when I didn't believe entirely in myself. She took me under her wing and guided and encouraged me through the process of becoming an author. When Rebecca set off on her own *Eat, Pray, Love* adventure, she entrusted me to the extremely capable hands of Dorian Karchmar,

who motivated me every day with her smarts and boundless energy. A girl couldn't be more fortunate to have these two women in her life.

Rebecca and Dorian's determination to sell this book brought me to my sweet-as-pie editor, Cassie Jones, who I only wish lived 3000 miles closer. Cassie, from the moment I walked into your office I felt as if all roads had been leading to you all along. Every day I am awed by the depths of your intelligence, taste, style, grace, and passion. Every author should experience the good fortune of an editor like you. I am truly blessed. Thank you for making this ride such an entertaining, enlightening, and gentle one, for supporting my choices through and through, and for always making every idea I have better than I imagined it could be. When I look through the pages of this book, I see you on every one. I have the utmost respect for you.

To the entire William Morrow team, who made everything come together so seamlessly in these pages: Jessica McGrady, Liate Stehlik, Lynn Grady, Shelby Meizlik, Tavia Kowalchuk, Megan Traynor, Shawn Nicholls, Kris Tobiassen,

Paula Szafranski, Joyce Wong, Ann Cahn, Karen Lumley, and Mary Schuck. Throughout this process I've learned how hard it is to put a book out into the world, yet you all make it look so easy.

The gorgeous images in the book would not be so, well, absolutely gorgeous without the boundless talent of Maren Caruso. Maren, you took my ideas and dreams and transformed them into the divine images in this book. I still smile (and drool) every time I look at them. Along with your partners in crime, Robyn Valarik and Jennifer Barguiarena, who used their magic style wands to pull our shoot all together, you chicks make the most divine trio. There's not a moment of food beauty you three cannot create, enhance, and capture.

To Josh B. and Chris J., the "Bosleys" in my world who continually guide and support me when I'm in uncharted waters.

To Alex. Thank you for your friendship, stovetop smarts, and always being my culinary 911.

To Alina, Sarah, Jacklene, and Katie, for standing at my side. Your energy and enthusiasm has always helped keep weelicious forging ahead.

To Rebecca, Brianne, Niki, and Erika (my gorgeous Brookettes). The first time we met you asked me what my dream was. Less than a year later it came true. You are without peer.

To Ming, my worldwide interweb guru. You helped give birth to and raise my third baby. To think that when you came into my life I could barely use e-mail. Weelicious would be a newsletter were it not for your guidance and expertise.

To Mike, my kitchen Tarantino. You've been with me since the beginning and showered your gifts on weelicious at 30 frames per second. Thank goodness I needed help using my computer that day, or heaven only knows what my cooking videos would look like.

To Robert, Aure, and CJ for your vision and for making me open my eyes much wider to see all the possibilities.

To all of my fellow bloggers who inspire me daily, I feel honored to know you and be a part of your community.

To Bit' z Kidz and Wean Green, who respectively donated some of the kids' clothes and food containers for our photo shoot. I adore your products because there's no substitute for beautiful design for kids. Visit them at www.bitzkidsnyc.com and www.weangreen.com.

To Audrey, August, Jack, Andrew and Matthew, Brown and Wolf, and Ruby, I couldn't ask for cuter models with better appetites to populate the pages of this book. It's true, I didn't pay you, but hey, you got to eat for free, so there.

To the Hollywood Farmers' Market and all the incredible vendors who come out every week, rain or shine, and whose food has graced my table for over a decade. Your warm smiles and friendship through the years has opened my family's eyes (and palates) to how real food should taste.

To Dan B, my hero and role model for inspiring kids to learn what farm to table really means.

To Dana. Thank you for your endless guidance. The greatest things that have happened in my life I owe to your wisdom. I'm blessed to know you.

To Nilva. You've always treated Kenya and Chloe as if they were your own. Your love for them and theirs for you is a priceless gift for me to witness every day. Not to mention, you're also the greatest taste tester out there!

To Kenya and Chloe's teachers: I am continuously amazed by what I observe every day in your classrooms. Your giving natures, generosity of time and spirit, and gentle methods of opening up worlds of possibilities for your kids have informed the way I interact with my own children in the kitchen, the garden, and life in general. I'm in awe of everything you do . . . and grateful for you allowing me to come share with the little ones in your care.

To my 24/7 cheerleading squad: Jillian, Jules, Juliet, Peyton, Jenny, Andrea, Cheryl, Jenno, the prettier J.G., Lizzie, Dana, Heather, Staci, Keri, Odessa, Naomi, Abby, Jenine, Sarah, Shandra, Rachel, Devon, Annika, Gail, Leslie, Diane, Lauri, Jenine, Jennifer, Maya, Jackie, Carla, Kelly, and "Downtown" Judi Brown. You'd all look damn cute in matching uniforms with pom-poms.

To my loving grandparents, who from as early as I can remember taught me about fresh food. Your open-door policy was incredibly empowering and unceasingly supportive. From taking me with you to pick fruits and vegetables at farms to allowing me to watch you cook more meals than I can recount, you're my heroes watching down from above.

To John, Paige, Sloane, Raleigh, Gant, Susan, Cathy, Jim, and all my adorable cousins: you're

the coolest cats I know, and no matter what, you've always encouraged me. You exemplify that there's nothing more important than family.

To Vivien and Sonny. I don't know what I did to deserve you. You've always taken care of me and treated me as if I was your own child. I admire you both for your strength and passion and for encouraging and inspiring me daily.

To Mom and Dad, who had no idea what to do with such an energetic child, but still allowed me to spread my wings and fly. You always told me I could do whatever I set my mind to, made me feel empowered, and supported me unconditionally. I'm endlessly proud of you for everything you've achieved and for the example you've set for me.

To Kenya and Chloe. You'll be my little babies forever, but watching you grow every day is the greatest miracle I could ever ask for. I'm so proud of who you are and who you will become, and for teaching me with every passing moment to be a better mother. I love you.

To Jon, my love, my best friend and life partner. You always support me without giving it an extra thought. I fell hard for you the day we met and have continued to do so every day since. I'm enamored by what an incredible father you are to our children and by how important you make all of us feel. I love knowing that I get to spend the rest of my life with you. I can ask you for nothing more . . . but knowing me, I probably will!

index

Note: Page references in *italics* indicate recipe photographs.

A

Apple(s)
-Cinnamon Sticks, 124, *125*
Oat Bars, 136, *137*
Roast, -Ginger Puree, 55
Streusel Oatmeal, Slow-Cooker, 68
-Vanilla Pancakes, 86–87, *87*
-Walnut Cookies, 251
Avocado(s)
Big Kid Guacamole, 110
Dip, Fruity, *118,* 119
Lime Sauce, 111
Shake, 260, *261*

B

Bacon and Cheese Waffles, *82,* 83
Banana(s)
Avocado Shake, 260, *261*
Bread Cake, *238,* 239
-Corn Fritters, 84
Cream Ice Pops, 145, *145*
Green Monster Smoothie, 259, *259*
-Oat–Chocolate Chip Cookies,
248–49, *249*
PBRB "Waffle" Sammies, 138, *138*
Peanut Butter Muffins, 128, *129*

Roast, and Pear Puree, 52
Wee-eat Germ Muffins, 132–33
Barley, Mushroom, 222
Bars
Apple Oat, 136, *137*
Chocolate Rice Crisp-wee Treats,
240, *241*
Fruit and Oat, 243
Oatmeal On-the-Go, 76, *77*
Basil and Sun-Dried Tomato Pesto, 107
Bean(s). *See also* Green Beans; Lentil
Black, Cakes, 224, *225*
Chloe's Olive Hummus, 106
Edamame Salsa, 115, *115*
Four-, Slow-Cooker Chili, 96–97
Veg-wee Burgers, 182
White, and Red Beet Hummus, 104, *105*
Beet(s)
Cookies, Sweet, 246, *247*
Cupcakes, Chocolate Velvet,
244, *244*
Red, and White Bean Hummus, 104,
105
Veggie Smoothie, 263, *263*
Blackberry Agua Fresca, 264, *264*
Blueberry(ies)
-Lemon Whole Wheat Pancakes,
62, *63*
Red, White, and Blue Parfaits, 69, *69*
Bread. *See also* Muffins; Tortilla(s)
Egg in the Hole, 60, *61*
French Toast Sticks, 73
Stuffed French Toast, 74, *75*

Broccoli
"Eat Your Greens" Puree, 50, *51*
Pesto, 108
Veggie Nuggets, 210–11, *211*
Burgers
Chicken Satay, with Peanut-Coconut
Sauce, 202–3, *203*
Veg-wee, 182

C

Cabbage
Kiddie Slaw, 223
Cake, Banana Bread, *238,* 239
Carrot(s)
Cake Cookies, 252–53, *253*
"Eat Your Greens" Puree, 50, *51*
-Ginger Soup, *92,* 93
-Miso-Ginger Dressing, 112, *112*
-Pineapple Cupcakes with Cream
Cheese Icing, 236–37
Veggie Nuggets, 210–11, *211*
Veggie Smoothie, 263, *263*
Cereal, Brown Rice, *46, 47*
Cheese. *See also* Cream Cheese
and Bacon Waffles, *82,* 83
Baked Shells, 166–67
Baked Ziti, 195
BBQ Chicken Quesadilla, 183
Breakfast Pizza Pockets, 80–81
Breakfast Quesadilla, 70–71
Cheesy Chicken Taquitos, 178, *179*

Chicken Parmesan Wheels,
174, *175*
Cottage, Pancakes, 66–67
Lasagna Rolls, 169
Mac, and Chicken Bites,
180–81, *181*
Mac and, Rice-Cooker, 160
Mexican Enchiladas, 158–59
Mexican Lasagna, 184, *185*
and Rice Treasures, 219, *219*
Ricotta Veggie Dip, 114
Spaghetti Pie, 204
Spanakopita Bites, 220–21, *221*
Spinach Ricotta Bites, 216, *217*
Sweet Noodles, 142, *142*
Chicken
BBQ, Quesadilla, 183
BBQ, Shredded, Sammies, 171
BBQ, Slow-Cooker, 170
Bok Choy Lo Mein, 207
Italian Pasta Pie, 198, *199*
Italian Wedding Soup, 98–99, *99*
Mac, and Cheese Bites, 180–81, *181*
Mexican Enchiladas, 158–59
Mexican Lasagna, 184, *185*
Noodle Soup, 100
Orange, 189
Parmesan Wheels, 174, *175*
and Rice Stir-Fry, 200
Satay Burgers with Peanut-Coconut
Sauce, 202–3, *203*
on a Stick, 156–57, *157*
Taquitos, Cheesy, 178, *179*
Tenders, Un-Fried, 161, *161*
Teriyak-wee, 168
Tortilla Soup, 90–91
and Wild Rice Casserole, 196
Wonton Soup, 94, *95*
Chili, Four-Bean Slow-Cooker, 96–97
Chocolate
Chip–Banana-Oat Cookies, 248–49,
249
–Peanut Butter Pudding, 242,
242
Rice Crisp-wee Treats, 240, *241*
Velvet Beet Cupcakes, 244, *244*
Cinnamon
-Honey Cookies, *254*, 255
-Honey Milk, 266, *266*
-Honey Popcorn, 139, *139*

Coconut
Date-Nut Bites, 143
Fruit and Seed Granola, 85
-Peanut Sauce, Chicken Satay
Burgers with, 202–3, *203*
-Pineapple Pops, 146, *147*
–Sweet Potato Puree, 49, *49*
Cookies
Apple-Walnut, 251
Banana-Oat–Chocolate Chip, 248–49,
249
Carrot Cake, 252–53, *253*
Graham Crackers, 122–23, *123*
Honey-Cinnamon, *254*, 255
PB&J Oatmeal Thumbprint, 250
Sweet Beet, 246, *247*
The Teething, 56, *57*
Cooking with kids
avoiding short-order cook
syndrome, 33
basic kitchen gear, 33–35
getting kids involved, 25–27
infants, 27–28
preschoolers, 28–30
school-age kids, 30–31
stocking the pantry, 36–37
Corn-Banana Fritters, 84
Corn Dog Bites on a Stick, *186*, 187
Corn Kernels, Italian, 212, *212*
Cornmeal
Banana-Corn Fritters, 84
Corn Dog Bites on a Stick, *186*, 187
Crackers
Apple-Cinnamon Sticks, 124, *125*
Graham, 122–23, *123*
Whole Wheat Seed, 126
Cream Cheese
Banana Cream Ice Pops, 145, *145*
Breakfast Cupcake "Frosting," 65, *65*
Frosting, 245
Icing, Carrot-Pineapple Cupcakes
with, 236–37
Parsnip Muffins, 130, *131*
–Raspberry Heart Tarts, 232–34, *233*
Stuffed French Toast, 74, *75*
Cupcakes
Breakfast, 64–65, *65*
Carrot-Pineapple, with Cream
Cheese Icing, 236–37
Chocolate Velvet Beet, 244, *244*

D

Date(s)
Apple Oat Bars, 136, *137*
Banana-Oat–Chocolate Chip
Cookies, 248–49, *249*
-Nut Bites, 143
Desserts. *See also* Bars; Cookies;
Cupcakes
Banana Bread Cake, *238*, 239
Chocolate–Peanut Butter Pudding,
242, *242*
Raspberry–Cream Cheese Heart
Tarts, 232–34, *233*
Dips
Avocado Lime Sauce, 111
Big Kid Guacamole, 110
Broccoli Pesto, 108
Chloe's Olive Hummus, 106
Edamame Salsa, 115, *115*
Fruity Avocado, *118*, 119
Honey-Mustard Dipping Sauce, 215,
215
Ranch, 113
Red Beet and White Bean Hummus,
104, *105*
Ricotta Veggie, 114
Sun-Dried Tomato and Basil Pesto, 107
Dressing, Carrot-Miso-Ginger, 112, *112*
Drinks
Avocado Shake, 260, *261*
Blackberry Agua Fresca, 264, *264*
Cinnamon-Honey Milk, 266, *266*
Ginger-Lemon-Honey Tea, 265, *265*
Green Monster Smoothie, 259, *259*
Strawberr-Wee Lemonade, 260
Veggie Smoothie, 263, *263*

E

Edamame Salsa, 115, *115*
Egg(s)
Baby Frittatas, 72
Breakfast Pizza Pockets, 80–81
Breakfast Quesadilla, 70–71
in the Hole, 60, *61*
Italian Pasta Pie, 198, *199*
Vegetable Frittata, 172, *173*
Enchiladas, Mexican, 158–59

F

Farmers' markets, 19–20
Feeding the kids
  avoiding food fights, 6–8
  buying healthy, whole foods, 10–14
  disguising fruits and vegetables,
    8–10
  don't impose dislikes or opinions,
    14–15
  giving kids some choice, 39–40
  homemade baby food, 3–4
  introducing new foods, 4–6
  making food fun, 40–41
  sharing family meals, 41
  starting solid foods, 3–4
Fish. *See also* Shrimp
  BBQ Salmon, 201, *201*
  Miso Marinated Fish, 194
  Salmon Noodle Casserole, 205
  Sweet Broiled Salmon, 197
Frittata, Vegetable, 172, *173*
Frittatas, Baby, 72
Fritters, Banana-Corn, 84
Frosting, Cream Cheese, 245
"Frosting," Breakfast Cupcake,
  65, *65*
Fruit. *See also specific fruits*
  and Oat Bars, 243
  Oatmeal On-the-Go Bars, 76, *77*
  organic, buying, 22–23
  and Seed Granola, 85
  Tropical, Salad, 151

G

Ginger
  -Carrot-Miso Dressing, 112, *112*
  -Carrot Soup, *92*, 93
  -Lemon-Honey Tea, 265, *265*
Gnocchi, Spinach, 226–27, *227*
Graham Crackers, 122–23, *123*
Grains. *See also* Cornmeal; Oat(s); Rice;
    Wheat germ
  Breakfast Polenta, 78
  Mushroom Barley, 222
  Veg-wee Burgers, 182
Granola, Fruit and Seed, 85
Granola Balls, Chewy, 140, *141*

Green Beans
  "Eat Your Greens" Puree, 50, *51*
  "Fried," with Honey-Mustard
    Dipping Sauce, 214–15, *215*
Greens. *See* Kale; Spinach

I

Ice Pops
  Banana Cream, 145, *145*
  Coconut-Pineapple Pops, 146, *147*
  Mango Pops, *148*, 149
  Pea Pops, 150, *150*
  Strawberry, 144, *145*

K

Kale
  Italian Wedding Soup, 98–99, *99*
  Lentil Vegetable Puree, 54
  Slow-Cooker Lentil Veggie Stew, 101
Kitchen cooking staples, 36–37
Kitchen equipment, 33–35

L

Lasagna, Mexican, 184, *185*
Lasagna Rolls, 169
Lemon(s)
  -Ginger-Honey Tea, 265, *265*
  Strawberr-Wee Lemonade, 260
Lentil Vegetable Puree, 54
Lentil Veggie Stew, Slow-Cooker, 101

M

Mango
  Fruity Avocado Dip, *118*, 119
  Pops, *148*, 149
  Tropical Fruit Salad, 151
Meat. *See also* Pork
  Corn Dog Bites on a Stick, *186*, 187
  Meatballs, Turkey Pesto, 164, *165*
  Meatloaf, Mexican Turkey, 206, *206*
  Miso-Carrot-Ginger Dressing, 112, *112*
  Miso Marinated Fish, 194

Muffins
  Banana Peanut Butter, 128, *129*
  Banana Wee-eat Germ, 132–33
  Parsnip, 130, *131*
  Sweet Potato, *134*, 135
Mushroom Barley, 222

N

Nuts. *See also* Walnut(s)
  Oatmeal On-the-Go Bars, 76, *77*

O

Oat(s)
  Apple Bars, 136, *137*
  -Banana-Chocolate Chip Cookies,
    248–49, *249*
  Fruit and Seed Granola, 85
  and Fruit Bars, 243
  Oatmeal On-the-Go Bars, 76, *77*
  PB&J Oatmeal Thumbprint Cookies,
    250
  Slow-Cooker Apple Streusel
    Oatmeal, 68
  Sweet Potato Muffins, *134*, 135
Olive Hummus, Chloe's, 106
Orange Chicken, 189
Organic foods, 21–23

P

Pancakes
  Apple-Vanilla, 86–87, *87*
  Blueberry-Lemon Whole Wheat, 62, *63*
  Cottage Cheese, 66–67
Parsnip Muffins, 130, *131*
Pasta and noodles
  Baked Shells, 166–67
  Baked Ziti, 195
  Chicken Bok Choy Lo Mein, 207
  Chicken Noodle Soup, 100
  Cold Sesame Soba Noodles, 192, *193*
  Four-Bean Chili Mac and Cheese, 97
  Four-Bean Chili Spaghetti, 97
  Italian Pasta Pie, 198, *199*
  Italian Wedding Soup, 98–99, *99*

Lasagna Rolls, 169
Mac, Chicken, and Cheese Bites,
    180–81, *181*
Rice-Cooker Mac and Cheese, 160
Salmon Noodle Casserole, 205
Spaghetti Pie, 204
Spinach Gnocchi, 226–27, *227*
Sweet Noodles, 142, *142*
Peanut Butter
    Banana Muffins, 128, *129*
    Chewy Granola Balls, 140, *141*
    Chicken Satay Burgers with Peanut-
        Coconut Sauce, 202–3, *203*
    –Chocolate Pudding, 242, *242*
    Chocolate Rice Crisp-wee Treats,
        240, *241*
    PB&J Oatmeal Thumbprint Cookies,
        250
    PBRB "Waffle" Sammies, 138, *138*
Pear, Roast, and Banana Puree, 52
Pea(s)
    "Eat Your Greens" Puree, 50, *51*
    and Mint Puree, 53, *53*
    Pops, 150, *150*
    Potato Cakes, 213, *213*
Pesto, Broccoli, 108
Pesto, Sun-Dried Tomato and Basil, 107
Pesto Turkey Meatballs, 164, *165*
Pie, Italian Pasta, 198, *199*
Pie, Spaghetti, 204
Pie Crust, Double, 235
Pineapple
    -Carrot Cupcakes with Cream
        Cheese Icing, 236–37
    Chicken Teriyak-wee, 168
    -Coconut Pops, 146, *147*
Polenta, Breakfast, 78
Popcorn, Cinnamon-Honey, 139, *139*
Pork
    Bacon and Cheese Waffles, *82*, 83
    Pulled, Slow-Cooker, Tacos,
        190–91
Potato(es). *See also* Sweet Potato(es)
    Baked, Four-Bean Chili, 97
    Four-Bean Chili Fries, 97
    Oven-Baked "Fries," 218, *218*
    Pea Cakes, 213, *213*
    Veggie Nuggets, 210–11, *211*
Poultry. *See* Chicken; Turkey
Pumpkin Waffles, 79

Q
Quesadilla, BBQ Chicken, 183
Quesadilla, Breakfast, 70–71

R
Raspberry(ies)
    –Cream Cheese Heart Tarts, 232–34,
        233
    PBRB "Waffle" Sammies, 138, *138*
    Raspberr-Wee Sauce, 117
    Red, White, and Blue Parfaits, 69, *69*
    Stuffed French Toast, 74, *75*
Rice
    Brown, and Veggie Casserole,
        162–63, *163*
    Brown, Cereal, *46*, 47
    and Cheese Treasures, 219, *219*
    and Chicken Stir-Fry, 200
    Shrimp "Fried," 188
    Wild, and Chicken Casserole, 196
Rice Crisp-wee Treats, Chocolate, 240,
    241

S
Salad, Tropical Fruit, 151
Salmon, BBQ, 201, *201*
Salmon, Sweet Broiled, 197
Salmon Noodle Casserole, 205
Salsa, Edamame, 115, *115*
Sandwiches
    PBRB "Waffle" Sammies, 138, *138*
    Shredded BBQ Chicken Sammies, 171
Sauces
    Avocado Lime, 111
    Honey-Mustard Dipping, 215, *215*
    Raspberr-Wee, 117
    Tomato, Weelicious, 116
Seed(s)
    Crackers, Whole Wheat, 126
    and Fruit Granola, 85
    Oatmeal On-the-Go Bars, 76, *77*
    Sunflower Seed Brittle, 127, *127*
Shopping with kids
    buying organic foods, 21–23
    farmers' markets, 19–20

money-saving strategies, 20–21
    tips for, 17–19
    top inexpensive, nutritious foods, 21
Shrimp "Fried" Rice, 188
Shrimp Tacos, *176*, 177
Slaw, Kiddie, 223
Soups
    Carrot-Ginger, *92*, 93
    Chicken Noodle, 100
    Chicken Tortilla, 90–91
    Chicken Wonton, 94, *95*
    Italian Wedding, 98–99, *99*
Spanakopita Bites, 220–21, *221*
Spinach
    Chicken Parmesan Wheels, 174, *175*
    Gnocchi, 226–27, *227*
    Green Monster Smoothie, 259, *259*
    Lasagna Rolls, 169
    Ricotta Bites, 216, *217*
    Spanakopita Bites, 220–21, *221*
Squash. *See also* Zucchini
    Butternut, Puree, 48
    Pumpkin Waffles, 79
Stews
    Four-Bean Slow-Cooker Chili, 96–97
    Slow-Cooker Lentil Veggie, 101
Strawberry(ies)
    Fruit Leather, 152–53, *153*
    Ice Pops, 144, *145*
    Strawberr-Wee Lemonade, 260
Sweet Potato(es)
    –Coconut Puree, 49, *49*
    "Eat Your Greens" Puree, 50, *51*
    Muffins, *134*, 135

T
Tacos, Shrimp, *176*, 177
Tacos, Slow-Cooker Pulled Pork,
    190–91
Taquitos, Cheesy Chicken, 178, *179*
Tarts, Raspberry–Cream Cheese Heart,
    232–34, *233*
Tofu
    Cold Sesame Soba Noodles, 192, *193*
Tomato(es)
    Baked Ziti, 195
    Sauce, Weelicious, 116
    Sun-Dried, and Basil Pesto, 107

Tortilla(s)
  BBQ Chicken Quesadilla, 183
  Breakfast Quesadilla, 70–71
  Cheesy Chicken Taquitos, 178, *179*
  Mexican Enchiladas, 158–59
  Mexican Lasagna, 184, *185*
  Shrimp Tacos, *176*, 177
  Slow-Cooker Pulled Pork Tacos,
    190–91
  Soup, Chicken, 90–91
Turkey
  Baked Shells, 166–67
  Meatloaf, Mexican, 206, *206*
  Pesto Meatballs, 164, *165*
  Spaghetti Pie, 204

V

Vegetable(s). *See also specific*
    vegetables
  Brown Rice and Veggie Casserole,
    162–63, *163*

Frittata, 172, *173*
Lentil Puree, 54
organic, buying, 22–23
Slow-Cooker Lentil Veggie Stew, 101
Veggie Nuggets, 210–11, *211*
Veggie Smoothie, 263, *263*
Veg-wee Burgers, 182

W

Waffles
  Bacon and Cheese, *82*, 83
  PBRB "Waffle" Sammies, 138, *138*
  Pumpkin, 79
Walnut(s)
  -Apple Cookies, 251
  Carrot Cake Cookies, 252–53, *253*
  Date-Nut Bites, 143
  Slow-Cooker Apple Streusel
    Oatmeal, 68

Wheat germ
  Banana Wee-eat Germ Muffins,
    132–33
  Fruit and Seed Granola, 85
Wild Rice and Chicken Casserole, 196

Y

Yogurt
  Chocolate–Peanut Butter Pudding,
    242, *242*
  Ranch Dip, 113
  Red, White, and Blue Parfaits, 69, *69*

Z

Zucchini
  Coins, Baked, *228*, 229
  Ricotta Veggie Dip, 114